Flags of the World

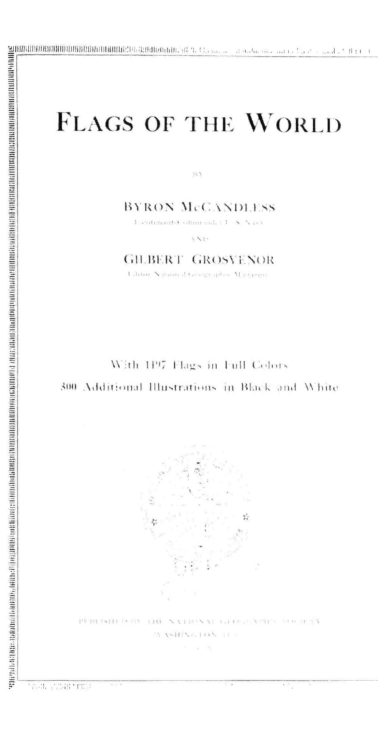

Flags of the World

BY

BYRON McCANDLESS

Lieutenant Commander, U. S. Navy

AND

GILBERT GROSVENOR

Editor National Geographic Magazine

With 1197 Flags in Full Colors

300 Additional Illustrations in Black and White

PUBLISHED BY THE NATIONAL GEOGRAPHIC SOCIETY

WASHINGTON, D. C.

U. S. A.

Washington
Press of Judd & Detweiler, Inc
1917

THE WHITE HOUSE
WASHINGTON

14 December, 1917

My dear Mr. Grosvenor:

The Flag Number of the National Geographic Magazine is indeed most interesting and most valuable. I sincerely congratulate you on the thoroughness and intelligence with which the work has been done. It constitutes a very valuable document indeed.

Cordially and sincerely yours,

Woodrow Wilson

Mr. Gilbert H. Grosvenor, Director,
National Geographic Society.

THE SECRETARY OF THE NAVY

WASHINGTON

December 3, 1917

My dear Mr. Grosvenor:

I wish to congratulate and thank you for the magnificent Flag Number of the National Geographic Magazine. It had for me a personal as well as a national interest, because during the weeks that Lieutenant Commander Byron McCandless was busy in the preparation of the articles and the flags which adorn the magazine I caught something of the spirit of enthusiasm and patriotism which marked the delightful labor which he brought to the study and preparation of what is truly an historic number. To have given to the people a beautiful Flag Number at any time would have been in keeping with the educational service which the National Geographic Magazine has long rendered to the American public. To have given this service at this time, when the Flag means more to us than ever before in our history, and when millions of young men are responding cheerfully to its call because of the principles it symbolizes, your Flag Number may be truly said to be a contribution to the victory which will be won under the inspiration of the ideals which the Flag embodies.

Sincerely yours,

Mr. Gilbert H. Grosvenor, Editor,
The National Geographic Magazine,
Washington, D. C.

THE SECRETARY OF WAR

WASHINGTON

December 12, 1917

My dear Mr. Grosvenor

I am very glad to have the second copy of the Flag Issue of the National Geographic Magazine which you were good enough to send me, the first having already reached me at my home, and I wish to thank you on behalf of my associates in the War department for the Society's generous offer to present a special edition of 5000 copies of the magazine for the use of the men in the Army.

This issue is not only of general interest, as all the issues of the magazine are, but of permanent value for reference, and of particular usefulness to the men in the military service of the United States at this time.

With best wishes and renewed thanks, I am

Cordially yours,

Mr. Gilbert H. Grosvenor, Editor,
The National Geographic Magazine,
Washington D. C.

THE NATIONAL GEOGRAPHIC SOCIETY

THE FLAG BOOK

FLAGS [illegible]

Photograph by U. S. Navy Department

ON REVIEW

The seamen, spaced equally distant, are manning the rail, a part of the ceremony when the President or a sovereign passes a ship of the navy. The national ensign (1) is flying at the stern and the jack (4) at the bow.

Photograph by [illegible]

THE PRESIDENT OF THE UNITED STATES ON BOARD A BARGE WHICH FLIES HIS FLAG AT THE BOW WHILE TAKING HIM FROM THE "MAYFLOWER" TO THE FLAGSHIP (SEE ALSO PAGE 324)

The President's flag (No. 2, page 300) is one of the most difficult flags to make, requiring the labor of a skilled seamstress for an entire month. Every detail of the eagle, [illegible] the stars and each scale, must be carefully [illegible] rendered. [illegible] the year the ships of the American Navy are "full dressed," as are the [illegible] ships shown here. These occasions are the Fourth of July, the birthday of the nation itself, and the Twenty-second of February, the birthday of him who will ever remain first in the hearts of his countrymen. The "full dress ship" is also permissible as a matter of international courtesy, when in foreign ports, [illegible] presence of [illegible]

standing and appreciating the motives, the traditions, and the sentiments which have given birth to these various symbols of sovereignty, the National Geographic Society presents this work, devoted to the flags of all countries.

In the present world struggle, in which the United States of America is now engaged, we of this land hold to the ideals represented in the history and the purpose of the Stars and Stripes—the ideals of life, liberty, and the pursuit of happiness safeguarded for all mankind.

And though many must fall in the achievement of those ideals, a noble and imperishable good will endure as a monument to their sacrifice. History can bestow upon soldiers no higher [illegible] occasion than that of [illegible] defenders of the Flag.

In presenting 1,197 flags in accurate colors and designs, the plates of which [illegible] to this number, the Society [illegible] the most expensive, instructive, and beautiful number of its magazine in the history of periodical literature.

[illegible]

[illegible] the flags of the world [illegible] [illegible]

GEOGRAPHIC SOCIETY has been fortunate in having the enthusiastic cooperation and active professional services of the foremost flag expert of the United States Government and probably the leading authority in the world on flag usages among maritime nations—Lieut. Commander Byron McCandless, of the United States Navy.

Lieut. Commander McCandless was the flag officer of the American fleet at Vera Cruz in 1913, and in the performance of his duties there he found that the signal officers and enlisted men were handicapped in their work by the non-existence of a flag book. Being far removed from a printing establishment, the ingenious officer met the condition by chiseling flag plates from leaden sheets and printing in color a book of flags with a hand-press installed on the flagship. This unique publication attracted wide attention among naval officers, and the demand for copies of the work became so great that the improvised flag plates, made of soft metal, soon wore away.

Lieut. Commander McCandless was induced by the NATIONAL GEOGRAPHIC SOCIETY to undertake, with the consent of the Secretary of the Navy, the assembling of the flags of the world for this volume. In view of the value of this flag material to the government, the SOCIETY has donated 5,000 copies of the Flag Book to the United States Navy and 5,000 copies to the Army.

In addition to the expert services of Lieut. Commander McCandless, the Editor has had the assistance of John Oliver La Gorce, the Associate Editor, of William Joseph Showalter, Ralph A. Graves, Franklin L. Fisher, and other members of the editorial staff in the months of research work necessary to secure the historically accurate data descriptive of the more than 1,200 flags in colors and in black and white. Thus through such concerted effort it is possible to present in this issue the most complete and authoritative work on flags ever published.

The engraving of the coats-of-arms and devices appearing on many of the banners and the preparation of all the color plates in their accurate proportions, as well as the notable achievement in rich color printing, have been accomplished through the mechanical efficiency and artistic cooperation of the Beck Engraving Company, of Philadelphia. In the processes of color printing it was necessary to operate the presses in daylight only, in order that the tints and shades might be kept true for each of the 23,000,000 pages (32 pages of color in each of more than 700,000 copies of the NATIONAL GEOGRAPHIC MAGAZINE).

The Flag Number and the Flag Book, like all the other issues since the founding of the magazine twenty-nine years ago, owe their attractive typographical appearance to Messrs. Judd & Detweiler, Inc., of Washington, D. C.

THE WORK OF PRINTING

So vast has grown the membership of the NATIONAL GEOGRAPHIC SOCIETY that one finds it hard to realize how widespread is the geographic interest it has engendered or how many magazines must be printed before each member can receive his or her copy. Two striking illustrations of the SOCIETY'S numerical strength have come home to the Editor in the issuance of the Flag Number. With one of the largest color printing plants in America engaged in producing the 32 pages of flags in colors, it took 75 working days—three months—to print these alone.

The attention of the reader is directed to the little vacant spaces after flags 640 and 660, respectively (pages 350-351). These blank intervals do not seem to be more than negligible, and yet, running through the entire edition of the NATIONAL GEOGRAPHIC MAGAZINE, they occupy more than 700,000 square inches of space, or 1,728 pages. Put side by side, they would form a ribbon of paper twenty miles long.

GILBERT GROSVENOR,
Editor and Director,
National Geographic Society.

INDEX TO FLAGS AND INSIGNIA

[illegible]

[illegible]

THE STORY OF THE AMERICAN FLAG

AS IF in augury of that perpetual peace for which all mankind hopes as the outcome of the world war, immediately following the entrance of the United States of America into the great struggle to secure democracy for all peoples and freedom from the menace of militarism for all nations, the Stars and Stripes were received gratefully and reverently into that historic shrine of the English-speaking race—St. Paul's Cathedral, London—there to be preserved among the hallowed banners of the hosts of liberty (see page 302).

This epochal event marked the alliance, in a sacred cause, of the two great self-governing Anglo-Saxon nations just 140 years after the birth of that Star Spangled Banner in the travail of the conflict which severed the American Republic from the British Empire.

From the embattled pinnacle of high resolve and lofty idealism where the American flag has always floated, the course of its rise may be surveyed—an inspiration to the patriot, an enduring emblem of hope for the oppressed. The story of the Stars and Stripes is the story of the nation itself; the evolution of the flag is symbolic of the evolution of our free institutions; its development epitomizes the amazing expansion of our boundaries and the development of our natural resources; its glorious history is the history of the people whose sovereignty it signifies.

In the embryonic days of the republic, when the Thirteen Original States were still feeble British colonies bordering the western shores of the Atlantic, there were almost as many varieties of banners borne by the Revolutionary forces as there are today races fused into one liberty-loving American people.

The local flags and colonial devices (Nos. 361-366, 377-422) displayed in battle on land and sea during the first months of the American Revolution proclaimed the attitude of the people of the several colonies in their grievances against the Mother Country.

When Bunker Hill and Lexington were fought, some of the staunchest patriots were still hopeful that an adjustment of the difficulties with the home government could be effected, and although on June 15, 1775, General Washington had been appointed commander-in-chief of the Continental forces raised, or to be raised, "for the defense of American liberty," the Continental Congress nearly a month later (July 8) addressed an appeal to King George in which the petitioners styled themselves "Your Majesty's faithful subjects."

DISINCLINED TO SEVER ALL TIES

Disinclined to sever all ties with England, yet bitterly resentful of the treatment accorded them and unyielding in their determination to resist further oppression, when it became necessary to adopt an ensign for their newly created navy, in the autumn of 1775, the revolting colonies chose a flag that reflected their feeling of unity with the Mother Country, but at the same time expressed their firm joint purpose to demand and obtain justice and liberty.

The events which resulted in the establishment of the Continental navy, and thereby the birth of the first flag representative of the thirteen united colonies, constitute one of the most picturesque chapters in American history. At the beginning of October the Continental Congress, sitting in Philadelphia, learned that two unarmed North Country-built brigs were sailing from England loaded with arms, powder, and other stores destined for Quebec. As the colonies were in sore need of powder and possessed neither factories for its manufacture nor ships for bringing it from abroad, Congress

THE BANNER UNDER WHICH [illegible] FOUGHT [illegible]

[illegible]

The [illegible] the sacrifice, theirs the honor, "nor shall their [illegible]"

instructed General Washington to apply to the Council of Massachusetts Bay for the two armed vessels in its service, to man them and to dispatch them with all speed in the hope of intercepting the munitions-laden brigs. The aid of the armed vessels of Rhode Island and Connecticut was also promised the commander-in-chief in this important enterprise.

General Washington, of his own initiative, had already purchased two vessels, which he had fitted out, officered with army captains, and manned with soldiers. These ships were the *Hannah* and the *Franklin*. By November 4 four additional cruisers had been added to the fleet—the *Lee*, the *Harrison*, the [illegible], and the [illegible].

Of this little fleet only the *Lee*, under command of John Manley, met with signal success in the bold undertaking. On November [illegible] it captured the brig [illegible] with a precious cargo of [illegible] 31 tons of musket shot, [illegible] several barrels of [illegible] brass mortar, subsequently called "Congress," which was to play an important part in forcing the evacuation of Boston.

One of the colonial ships, the [illegible] *Washington*, was captured [illegible] by H. M. S. [illegible], still in the Admiralty Office in London, are described as bearing a pale green pine tree in a field of white, [illegible] "An Appeal to Heaven" [illegible]. This flag was [illegible] under Washington's [illegible] the design having been suggested to the commander-in-chief by [illegible] Colonel Joseph Reed [illegible]

[illegible]

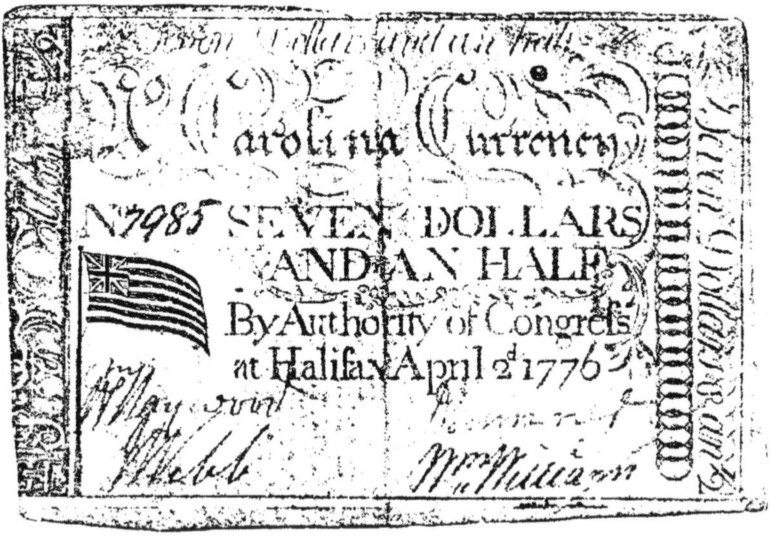

THE EARLIEST PERFECT REPRESENTATION OF THE GRAND UNION ENSIGN
(SEE NO. 364)

The flag is a part of the decorations appearing on North Carolina currency of the issue of April 2, 1776

Congress as distinguished from the soldier-manned fleet under General Washington. Immediately following his appointment Commodore Hopkins (the first and only commander-in-chief the navy ever had) set sail from Rhode Island in that colony's armed vessel *Katy* and arrived in the Delaware River on December 3, 1775. The same day the commodore assumed the formal command of the little squadron which the Congress had placed under him.

PAUL JONES RAISES THE FLAG

The manner in which that command was assumed is of signal importance, in that the ceremony marked the hoisting of the first truly American flag. And the distinction of having released the banner to the breeze belongs to that daring spirit, John Paul Jones, one of the chief among heroes in the hearts of American naval officers and seamen. Jones, at that time senior lieutenant (corresponding to executive officer in the navy today) of Hopkins' flagship, the *Alfred*, in a letter to "the United States Minister of Marine, Hon. Robert Morris," preserved in the Library of Congress, thus describes the historic event:

"It was my fortune, as the senior of the first Lieutenants, to hoist *myself* the Flag of America (I chose to do it with my own hands) the first time it was displayed. Though this was but a slight Circumstance, yet I feel for its Honor, more than I think I should have done, if it had not happened." A line is drawn through the words in parentheses and the word "myself" has been inserted.

This was the flag (364) which afterward figured so extensively in the literature of the day as the Congress Colors, from the fact that it first floated over the navy controlled by Congress. Also known as the Grand Union Flag and the First Navy Ensign, it was the Colonial standard from that day until it was superseded by the Stars and Stripes, in 1777. It consisted of thirteen stripes, alternately red and white, typifying the thirteen colonies, with a union bearing the crosses of St. George and St. Andrew combined (the national flag of Great Britain, 361) and signifying the Mother Country.

There has been much confusion about

the flags which were displayed on the *Alfred* on that historic December [illegible]. The statement is often made, [illegible] correctly, that Commodore Hopkins hoisted the Gadsden flag [illegible] which impresses some historians [illegible] of John Paul Jones [illegible] reference to naval usage [illegible] however [illegible] the supposed [illegible] flags [illegible] the flag of the commanding officer displayed at the mainmast [illegible] which flies from the [illegible]

The Gadsden flag [illegible] yellow silk [illegible] bearing a coiled rattlesnake [illegible] motto "Don't Tread on Me" [illegible] the *Alfred* as the flag of the commander commanding the fleet was presented [illegible] 8, 1776, to the Congress [illegible] Christopher Gadsden, a delegate from South Carolina to the Congress [illegible] and one of the committee of three [illegible] October 13, 1775, to [illegible] armed vessels [illegible] armed vessels.

The [illegible] displayed on the *Alfred* [illegible] the legend "Don't Tread on Me" [illegible] (365)

[illegible]

[illegible] Congress [illegible] Philadelphia [illegible] 1917 [illegible]

[illegible]

[illegible] *Alfred* [illegible] Congress [illegible] the Continental Congress [illegible] Washington [illegible] Cambridge [illegible] 1776 [illegible] Washington [illegible]

[illegible]

© Edward Moran

THE FIRST SALUTE TO THE STARS AND STRIPES

John Paul Jones, commanding the *Ranger*, fired a salute of 13 guns to the French fleet in Quiberon Bay on February 14, 1778, and received in return a salute of nine guns from Admiral La Motte Picquet, "the same salute authorized by the French court to be given an admiral of Holland or of any other republic." Thus was American independence first acknowledged in Europe (see page 301). The illustration is one of the famous marine paintings by Edward Moran in the National Museum, Washington, reproduced by courtesy of Theodore Sutro, New York.

© Harris & Ewing

THE FREMONT FLAG

When General John Charles Fremont, surnamed "the Pathfinder," made his way across the continent in the '40's, his mission was one of peace, but the arrows in his army flag suggested war to the Indians of the plain. Therefore he inserted the calumet, or pipe of peace, crossed with the arrows in the talons of the eagle. It is interesting to note that the army did not carry the Stars and Stripes until the period of the Mexican War (see pages 307-308 and flag 22).

Stripes (6), adopted by Congress a year and a half later, was carried in the field by the land forces during the Revolutionary War. The army carried only the colors of the States to which the troops belonged (see flags 394, 396, 403, 409, 410, etc.) and not the national flag.

THE FIRST VICTORY OF THE AMERICAN FLAG

It fell to the lot of the newly created Commodore Manley (the officer who had commanded the *Lee* and captured the ordnance ship *Nancy*) to carry the Grand Union Flag to its first victory. Commanding the *Hancock*, Manley captured two enemy transports, placed prize crews aboard, and then, with only 16 men left on his own ship, he engaged an armed vessel in sight of the enemy fleet at Boston and succeeded in bringing his prizes safely into Plymouth. Following this daring exploit Manley received a letter written at Cambridge, on January 28, 1776, by General Washington, who declared that the commodore's achievement merited "mine and the country's thanks," and promised him a "stronger vessel of war."

On Major Samuel Selden's powder-horn of that period is a carving showing Boston and vicinity. The British fleet is depicted on one side of Boston Neck, while Manley's symbolical ship *Amaraca*, flying at the stern the Continental Union flag as its ensign, and at the mainmast the pine-tree flag as the commodore's flag, is shown on the other side. The mortar carved on the horn is the famous "Congress" gun captured by Manley on the *Nancy*.

The first occasion upon which any American flag floated over foreign territory was on March 3, 1776. Commodore Hopkins, of the Congress fleet, organized an expedition against New Providence, in the Bahama Islands, for the purpose of seizing a quantity of powder known to be stored there and of which both General Washington and the fleet were in

U. S. S. "SYLPH" FLYING THE FOUR-STAR FLAG OF ADMIRAL BENSON, CHIEF OF NAVAL OPERATIONS (64), ON THE MAINMAST, AND THE FLAG OF VICE-ADMIRAL BROWNING, OF THE BRITISH NAVY (606), ON THE FOREMAST

Our naval jack (4) is flying at the jackstaff, but the motion of the steamer has given the stars a striped effect

great need. Two hundred marines were landed, under the command of Captain Nichols, supported by fifty sailors, under Lieutenant Weaver, of the *Cabot*. The *Providence* and the *Wasp* covered the landing party. Fort Nassau was taken and a great quantity of military stores fell into the hands of the expedition.

A correspondent of the London "Ladies' Magazine," who was in New Providence at the time of the capture of the fort by the American forces, under date of May 13, 1776, described the colors displayed by the marines and sailors as "striped under the union (the British union of the crosses of St. George and St. Andrew) with thirteen stripes" (364), while "the standard (the commodore's flag) bore a rattlesnake and the motto "Don't Tread on Me" (398).

THE FIRST FOREIGN SALUTE TO AN AMERICAN FLAG

The first salute ever fired in honor of an American flag (the Grand Union ensign) was an eleven-gun volley given by the Fort of Orange, on the island of St. Eustatius, Dutch West Indies, on November 16, 1776. The salute was in acknowledgment of a similar number of guns fired by the *Andrew Doria* (see also page 401), one of the original vessels of Commodore Hopkins' fleet, which had been sent to the West Indies, under command of Captain Isaiah Robinson, for a cargo of military supplies.

The commander of the near-by British island of St. Christopher, hearing of the salute, protested to the Dutch governor of St. Eustatius, Johannes de Graef, who promptly replied that "in regard to the reception given by the forts of this island, under my commandment, to the vessel *Andrew Doria*, I flatter myself that if my masters exact it I shall be able to give such an account as will be satisfactory." Whereupon the British commander responded that "the impartial world will judge between us whether these honor shots, answered on purpose by a Dutch fort to a rebellious brigantine, with a flag known to the commander of that fort as the flag of His Majesty's rebellious subjects, is or is not a partiality in favor of those rebels."

The British governor then forwarded

[illegible]

LAUNCHING THE U. S. S. "MICHIGAN"

In times of peace the launching of a battleship is made the occasion [illegible] ceremonies and witness of the enthusiastic throngs proud of the prowess [illegible] "take to the sea" of another man-of-war destined to uphold the honor of America. In times of war, however, no such crowds as attended the Michigan's launching are admitted to the shipyards, for an enemy might, with a bomb, undo the labor of years [illegible] our growing sea power.

to London a report of the affair, accompanied by affidavits that the brigantine "during the time of the salute and the answer to it, had the flag of the Continental Congress flying." The British Government protested sharply to the States General of the Republic of the Netherlands. The Dutch demurred at the asperity with which England demanded an explanation, but immediately recalled Commander de Graaf from St. Eustatius. Thus the first salute to the new ensign was disavowed, although the Holland Republic recognized American independence shortly thereafter.

In the literature of the Revolution frequent reference is found to a "plain striped flag" (1911). Official correspondence shows that whenever this flag was used afloat it was as the badge of merchant shipping and privateers and not as the ensign of the regular commissioned vessels of the navy. How long the Grand Union Flag was in use has never been definitely established; but official records of the navy fail to show that any other ensign was used until after the Star Spangled Banner's adoption by Congress.

[illegible]

It was nearly one year after the representatives of the United States of America, in General Congress assembled, had pledged their lives, their fortunes, and their sacred honor for the support of the Declaration of Independence [illegible] [illegible] of St. George and St. Andrew [illegible] of the North [illegible] Congress [illegible] [illegible] [illegible] "[illegible] in a blue field, representing a new constellation" (see flag No. 6, page 310).

The date [illegible] June 14, 1777 [illegible]

Photograph by Paul Thompson

COMMISSIONING THE U. S. S. "ARIZONA"

The ceremonies aboard a ship in commission when the ensign is raised and lowered are most impressive. At morning "colors" the band plays the national anthem and the flag is hoisted smartly. All officers face the ensign and salute and the guard of the day and the sentries present arms. At sunset "colors" the ensign is lowered slowly and with dignity as the national anthem is played, all officers and enlisted men facing the colors and saluting (see also pages 406-409).

Photograph by Paul Thompson

THE GUIDON, TROOP F, NEW YORK NATIONAL GUARD

Each troop of cavalry in the American forces carries a guidon—a small flag cut "swallow-tail" (23). It consists of two stripes of equal width, the upper being red, the cavalry colors, with the regimental designation in figures. The letter of the troop, in red, appears on the white stripe. Two guidons are supplied to each troop—a silken banner carried into battle, on campaigns, and upon occasions of ceremony, and a service flag of bunting to be used at all other times.

in the following letter to the Board of Admiralty more than a year later:

"GENTLEMEN: It is with great pleasure I understand my last device of a seal for the Board of Admiralty has met with your Honours' approbation. I have with great readiness upon several occasions exerted my small abilities in this way for the public service, as I flatter myself, to the satisfaction of those I wish to please, viz.,

The flag of the United States of America
4 Devices for the Continental currency
A Seal for the Board of Treasury
Ornaments, Devices and Checks, for the new bills of exchange on Spain and Holland.
A Seal for Ship Papers of the United States
A Seal for the Board of Admiralty
The Borders, Ornaments & Checks for the new Continental currency now in the press, a work of considerable length.
A Great Seal for the United States of America, with a Reverse.

"For these services I have as yet made

[illegible]

[illegible]

[illegible]

Rear Admiral [illegible]

[illegible]

© Underwood & Underwood

THE FRENCH ARMY'S FIRST SALUTE TO THE STARS AND STRIPES ON FRENCH SOIL

Section V-14 of the American Ambulance Corps, a team of Leland Stanford Jr. University students, had the honor of bearing the first American flag officially sent from the United States to the French front.

this vessel was a poor sailer and the wind had changed, the *Raleigh* went in alone, passing many merchant ships of the convoy. When within pistol-shot of the commodore's ship, recognized by means of the signal book, Thompson records:

"We up sails, out guns, hoisted Continental colours and bid them strike to the Thirteen United States. Sudden surprise threw them into confusion and their sails flew all aback, upon which we complimented them with a gun for each State, a whole broadside into their hull. Our second broadside was aimed at their rigging, which had its desired effect. In about a quarter of an hour all hands quitted quarters on board the British man-of-war; we cleared the decks totally. . . . Had not the wind favored him and we drifted leeward, he could not have fetched us and I should certainly have sunk the ship."

Thus occurred the baptism of fire at sea of the new flag, at the hour of sunset on September 4, 1777.

THE IMPROVISED OLD GLORY OF FORT STANWIX

Just one month previously (August 3) the new flag had been under fire on land, [illegible] Fort [illegible] of the present [illegible] August [illegible] [illegible] by Col. Peter [illegible] [illegible] Massachusetts Regiment [illegible] Colonel [illegible] the Mohawk River [illegible]

[illegible] and immediately the [illegible] make the new nation [illegible] ammunition shirts of the soldiers [illegible] the white stripes [illegible] the red stripes [illegible] [illegible]

In [illegible] the flag [illegible] [illegible] [illegible] the [illegible]

[illegible] the Continental [illegible] but the red [illegible] the humble soldiers [illegible] the Stars and Stripes [illegible]

[illegible]

[illegible]

[illegible] from Boston [illegible]

Photograph by Central News Photo Service

FLAGS WHICH SIGNALIZED AMERICA'S ENTRANCE INTO THE WORLD CONFLICT BEING BORNE INTO ST. PAUL'S CATHEDRAL BY THE FIRST AMERICAN TROOPS TO REACH LONDON AFTER THE DECLARATION OF WAR WITH GERMANY

These Stars and Stripes were blessed in the great English shrine and are to be preserved for all time, together with those of our Allies, whose national emblems, like our own, are waving over the hosts fighting for the world's liberty (see page 280).

"The stars upon it were like the bright morning stars of God, and the stripes upon it were beams of morning light. As at early dawn the stars shine forth even while it grows light, and then as the sun advances that light breaks into banks and streaming lines of color, the glowing red and intense white striving together, and ribbing the horizon with bars effulgent, so, on the American flag, stars and beams of many-colored light shine out together. And wherever this flag comes and men behold it they see in its sacred emblazonry no embattled castles or insignia of imperial authority; they see the symbols of light. It is the banner of Dawn."

BIBLICAL ORIGIN OF THE RED, WHITE, AND BLUE

Charles W. Stewart superintendent of naval records and library of the United

[illegible]

THE MAKERS OF THE FLAG*

By Franklin K. Lane, Secretary of the Interior

THIS morning, as I passed into the Land Office, The Flag dropped me a most cordial salutation, and from its rippling folds I heard it say: "Good morning, Mr. Flag Maker."

"I beg your pardon, Old Glory," I said, "aren't you mistaken? I am not the President of the United States, nor a member of Congress, nor even a general in the army. I am only a government clerk."

"I greet you again, Mr. Flag Maker," replied the gay voice; "I know you well. You are the man who worked in the swelter of yesterday straightening out the tangle of that farmer's homestead in Idaho, or perhaps you found the mistake in that Indian contract in Oklahoma, or helped to clear that patent for the hopeful inventor in New York, or pushed the opening of that new ditch in Colorado, or made that mine in Illinois more safe, or brought relief to the old soldier in Wyoming. No matter; whichever one of these beneficent individuals you may happen to be, I give you greeting, Mr. Flag Maker."

I was about to pass on, when The Flag stopped me with these words:

"Yesterday the President spoke a word that made happier the future of ten million peons in Mexico; but that act looms no larger on the flag than the struggle which the boy in Georgia is making to win the Corn Club prize this summer.

"Yesterday the Congress spoke a word which will open the door of Alaska; but a mother in Michigan worked from sunrise until far into the night to give her boy an education. She, too, is making the flag.

"Yesterday we made a new law to prevent financial panics, and yesterday, maybe, a school teacher in Ohio taught his first letters to a boy who will one day write a song that will give cheer to the millions of our race. We are all making the flag."

"But," I said impatiently, "these people were only working!"

Then came a great shout from The Flag:

"The work that we do is the making of the flag.

"I am not the flag; not at all. I am but its shadow.

"I am whatever you make me; nothing more.

"I am your belief in yourself, your dream of what a people may become.

"I live a changing life, a life of moods and passions, of heart-breaks and tired muscles.

"Sometimes I am strong with pride, when men do an honest work, fitting the rails together truly.

"Sometimes I droop, for then purpose has gone from me, and cynically I play the coward.

"Sometimes I am loud, garish, and full of that ego that blasts judgment.

"But always I am all that you hope to be and have the courage to try for.

"I am song and fear, struggle and panic, and ennobling hope.

"I am the day's work of the weakest man and the largest dream of the most daring.

"I am the Constitution and the courts, statutes and the statute-makers, soldier and dreadnaught, drayman and street sweep, cook, counselor, and clerk.

"I am the battle of yesterday and the mistake of tomorrow.

"I am the mystery of the men who do without knowing why.

"I am the clutch of an idea and the reasoned purpose of resolution.

"I am no more than what you believe me to be and I am all that you believe I can be.

"I am what you make me; nothing more.

"I swing before your eyes as a bright gleam of color, a symbol of yourself, the pictured suggestion of that big thing which makes this nation. My stars and my stripes are your dream and your labors. They are bright with cheer, brilliant with courage, firm with faith, because you have made them so out of your hearts; for you are the makers of the flag, and it is well that you glory in the making."

*Delivered on Flag Day, 1914, before the employees of the Department of the Interior, Washington, D. C.

THE FLAGS OF OUR ARMY, NAVY, AND GOVERNMENT DEPARTMENTS

borne on the breast of an American eagle without any other supporters, to denote that the United States ought to rely on their own virtue.

Reverse.—The pyramid signifies strength and duration. The eye over it and the motto allude to the many signal interpositions of Providence in favor of the American cause. The date underneath is that of the Declaration of Independence, and the words under it signify the beginning of the new American era, which commences from that date.

The reverse of the seal has never been cut and has been allowed to go unused officially to the present day.

USES OF THE GREAT SEAL

When the Continental Congress made the obverse of the great seal of the national arms it intended that the device should pass into common use among the people, as the flag has done, and like the flag, the arms at first met with general approval, which soon gave place to an acceptance of it as an emblem of the power and sovereignty of the United States.

The seal itself has, of course, a very limited use, which is strictly guarded by law. The Secretary of State is its custodian, but even he has no authority to affix it to any paper that does not bear the President's signature.

At the present time the seal of the United States is affixed to the commissions of all Cabinet officers and diplomatic and consular officers who are nominated by the President and confirmed by the Senate; all ceremonious communications from the President to the heads of foreign governments; all treaties, conventions, and formal agreements of the President with foreign powers; all proclamations by the President; all exequaturs to foreign consular officers in the United States who are appointed by the heads of the governments which they represent; to warrants by the President to receive persons surrendered by foreign governments under extradition treaties; and to all miscellaneous commissions of civil officers appointed by the President, by and with the advice and consent of the Senate, whose appointments are not now especially directed by law to be signed under a different seal.

4. JACK.—Vessels at anchor fly the union jack from the jackstaff (the staff at the bow) from morning to evening colors. The jack hoisted at the fore mast is a signal for a pilot (220). A gun may be fired to call attention to it. Hoisted at the mizzen mast or at a yard arm it denotes that a general court martial or a court of inquiry is in session.

When a diplomatic official of the United States of and above the rank of chargé d'affaires pays an official visit afloat in a boat of the navy, a union jack of a suitable size is carried on a staff in the bow. When the Naval Governor of Guam, Tutuila, or the Virgin Islands of the United States embarks in a boat, within the limits of his government, for the purpose of paying visits of ceremony in his official capacity as Governor, a union jack of suitable size is carried on a staff in the bow of the boat. The union jack at the main was the flag of the Secretary of the Navy from 1869 to July 4, 1874, when the present flag (49) came into use.

When worn out, jacks are surveyed and burned in the same manner as ensigns. The proper size of jack to display with an ensign is that corresponding in dimension to the union of that ensign (see drawing, page 312). Yachts may display the union jack while at anchor at the jackstaff from 8 a. m. to sunset, when wash clothes are not triced up.

5. SEAL OF THE PRESIDENT.—This is the personal seal of the President, and the press from which it is made has been in use for many years. The device is to be seen in the President's flag (2), in bronze, in the floor of the entrance corridor of the White House and in the favorite stick-pin of the President.

6. OUR FIRST STARS AND STRIPES, adopted by act of Congress June 14, 1777 (see page 297). In its resolution Congress did not direct a specific arrangement of the thirteen stars. In the navy it became customary to place the stars so as to form the crosses of St. George and St. Andrew, an arrangement distinctly illustrated in Rhode Island's banner (396).

THE FLAG THAT INSPIRED THE "STAR SPANGLED BANNER"

7. THE FLAG WITH 15 STRIPES AND 15 STARS.—When Vermont entered the Union (March 4, 1791), followed by Kentucky (June 1, 1792), it was felt that the new States should have the same representation in the design of the flag that the original thirteen States possessed, and Congress accordingly passed the following act, which was approved by President Washington on January 13, 1794:

"*Be it enacted, etc.*, That from and after the first day of May, one thousand seven hundred and ninety-five, the flag of the United States be fifteen stripes, alternate red and white, and that the Union be fifteen stars, white in a blue field."

In this flag the stars were arranged in three parallel rows of five each, with the blue field resting on the fifth red stripe. This was the national flag for twenty-three years. It was in use during the war of 1812, and, in September, 1814, waving over Fort McHenry, it inspired Francis Scott Key to write the "Star Spangled Banner." Key was aide to General Smith at Baltimore and had gone aboard H. M. S. *Minden* in the harbor to arrange an exchange of prisoners. While being detained pending the bombardment on the morning of September 14, 1814, he wrote the anthem.

The arrangement of the stars in the Fort McHenry flag is the navy arrangement, that particular flag of immense size having been specially made by Mrs. Mary Pickerskill under the direction of Commodore Barry and General Striker. The flag is now in the National Museum at Washington (see page 289). The missing star is said to have been cut out and sent to President Lincoln.

This is the flag that encouraged our brave lads in our war against the Barbary pirates. It was the first ensign to be hoisted over a fort of the Old World. On April 27, 1805, after a

GUARD OF THE STANDARD

of stars emblazoned thereon, with the designation of the body of troops (see 22).

In 1834 War Department regulations gave the artillery the right to carry the Stars and Stripes. The infantry still used the design of 22 until 1841 and the cavalry until 1887, when that branch of the army was ordered to carry the Stars and Stripes. The history of the flag indicates that the Stars and Stripes were not officially carried by troops in battle until the period of the Mexican War, 1846-1847.

THE ARMY FLAGS

The flags used by the United States Army to designate its several branches are divided into two classes—colors and standards. The colors are used by unmounted troops and the standards by mounted forces. The principal difference between them is that the standards are smaller and have no cords and tassels because large flags and cords and tassels would hinder the movements of the mounted standard-bearer.

Every regiment of engineers, artillery, infantry, cavalry, etc., is supplied with one silk national standard or color (17) and one silk regimental standard or color (11, 13, 15, 18, etc.).

The silk national and regimental colors or standards are carried in battle, campaign, and on all occasions of ceremony at regimental headquarters in which two or more companies of the regiment participate.

The official designation of the regiment is engraved on a silver band placed on the pike or lance.

When not in use, colors and standards are kept in their waterproof cases.

In garrison the standards or colors, when not in use, are kept in the office or quarters of the colonel and are escorted thereto and therefrom by the color guard. In camp the colors or standards, when not in use, are displayed in front of the colonel's tent, the national color or standard on the right. From reveille to retreat, when the weather permits, they are uncased; from retreat to reveille and during inclement weather they are cased.

In action the position of the standards or colors will be indicated by the colonel, who may, through their display, inspire enthusiasm and maintain the morale. He may, however, hold them back when they might indicate to the enemy the direction of the main attack, betray the position of the main body, or tend to commit the regiment to defensive action. In the presence of the enemy and during the approach the standards are carried cased ready to be instantly broken out if their inspiration is required.

In addition to the handsome silk flags, a national color or standard made of bunting or other suitable material, but in all other respects similar to the silk national color or standard, is furnished to each battalion or squadron of each regiment.

These colors and standards are for use at drills and on marches and on all service other than battles, campaigns, and occasions of ceremony. Not more than one national color or standard is carried when the regiment or any part of it is assembled.

The colors of a regiment will not be placed in mourning or draped except when ordered from the War Department. Two streamers of crape 7 feet long and about 12 inches wide attached to the ferrule below the spearhead will be used for the purpose.

The names and dates of battles in which regiments or separate battalions have participated are engraved on silver bands and placed on the pike of the colors or lance of the standard of the regiment or separate battalion, as the case may be. For this purpose only the names of those battles which conform to the following definition are considered, viz: Battles are important engagements between independent armies in their own theaters of war, in contradistinction to conflicts in which but a small portion of the opposing forces are actually engaged, the latter being called, according to their nature, affairs, combats, skirmishes, and the like.

The names and dates of battles which it is proposed to have engraved on the silver bands are submitted to the War Department, which decides each case on its merits.

At least two companies, troops, or batteries of a regiment or separate battalion must have participated in a battle in order that the name of the battle may be placed on its colors or standards.

A company, troop, or battery does not receive credit for having participated in a battle unless at least one-half of its actual strength was engaged.

The Adjutant General of the Army furnishes each company, troop, and battery with a suitably engrossed certificate setting forth the names of all battles, engagements, and minor affairs in which said company, troop, or battery participated, with the dates thereof, and showing, as nearly as may be, the organizations of the United States troops engaged therein, and against what enemy. This certificate states that the names and dates of these battles are engraved on silver bands on the pike of the colors of the regiment or battalion, or the lance of the standard of the regiment or battalion, as the case may be, excepting in the case of companies which have no regimental or battalion organization.

This certificate is suitably framed and kept posted in the barracks of the company, troop, or battery.

Whenever in the opinion of a commanding officer the condition of any silk color, standard, or guidon in the possession of his command has become unserviceable, the same is forwarded to the depot quartermaster, Philadelphia, Pa., for repair if practicable. Should it be found that its condition does not warrant the expenditure of funds that may be involved, the depot quartermaster returns to the officer from whom received and furnishes a new color, standard, or guidon.

Upon receipt of new silk colors, standards, or guidons, commanding officers cause those replaced to be numbered and retained by the organization to which they belong as mementos of service, a synopsis of which bearing the same number will be filed with the records of the organization.

1 U S FLAG AND ENSIGN

2 PRESIDENT'S FLAG

3 GREAT SEAL—U S A

4 JACK

5 PRESIDENT'S SEAL

6 FLAG—JUNE 14 1777

7 FLAG—MAY 1 1795 (FT McHENRY FLAG)

8 FLAG—JULY 4 1818

PRESIDENT'S COLORS

INFANTRY COLORS

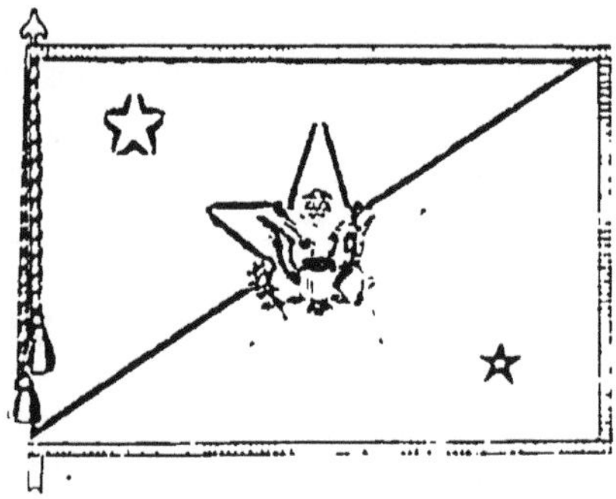

UNITED STATES ENSIGN

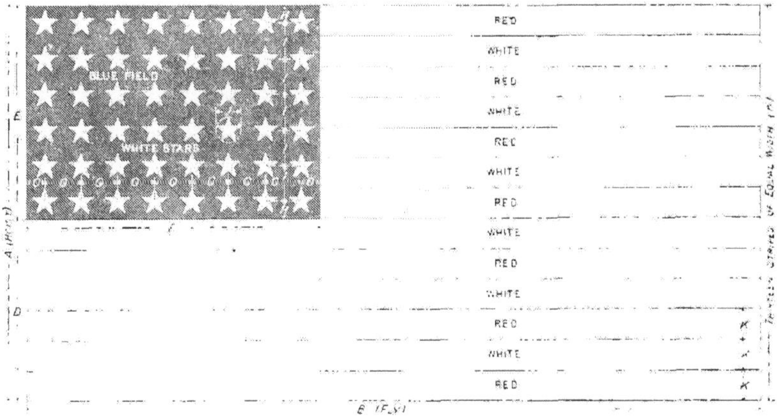

No	A	B	C	D	E	F	G	H	I	J	K
	FEET	FEET	FEET	FEET	FEET	FEET	FEET	FOOT	FEET	FEET	FEET
1	20	38	.95	9.23	10.77	15.20	1.90	.897	1.70	1.23	1.54
2	19	36.10	.903	8.77	10.23	14.44	1.81	.850	1.70	1.17	1.46
3	14.35	27.27	.619	6.62	7.73	10.01	1.24	.642	1.28	.883	1.103
4	12.19	23.16	.579	5.63	6.56	9.26	1.16	.545	1.09	.751	.935
5	10	19	.475	4.62	5.38	7.60	.95	.449	.90	.616	.769
6	8.94	16.99	.424	4.13	4.81	6.79	.848	.400	.798	.551	.687
7	5.14	9.77	.244	2.37	2.77	3.91	.488	.230	.459	.317	.395
8	5	9.50	.237	2.31	2.69	3.80	.475	.224	.449	.308	.385
9	3.52	6.69	.167	1.62	1.90	2.68	.335	.158	.316	.271	.271
10	2.90	5.51	.138	1.34	1.56	2.20	.275	.130	.260	.20[illegible]	.223
11	2.37	4.50	.113	1.09	1.28	1.80	.225	.106	.212	.167	.152
12	1.31	2.49	.062	.60	.71	1.00	.124	.059	.118	.094	.101

ARMY SIZES
Nos. 1, 5 and 8

BOAT FLAG SIZES
Nos. 9, 10, 11 and 12

FOREIGN ENSIGNS

No.	A	B
	FEET	
1	13.12	VARIABLE
2	8.75	VARIABLE

UNION JACK

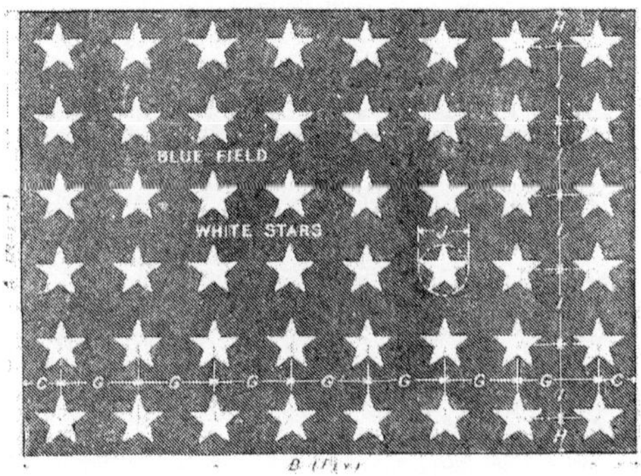

UNION JACK

No.	A	B	C	H	I	G	J
	FEET	FEET	FOOT	FOOT	FEET	FEET	FEET
2	10.23	14.44	.902	.850	1.705	1.805	1.170
3	7.72	10.91	.619	.642	1.281	1.238	.883
4	6.56	9.26	.579	.545	1.089	1.158	.751
6	4.51	6.79	.424	.400	.798	.848	.551
7	2.77	3.91	.244	.230	.459	.488	.317

No	SECRETARY OF THE NAVY (SEE FLAGS 47 & 53) A	B	ADMIRAL, VICE ADMIRAL ETC (SEE FLAGS 64 TO 66) A	B	SENIOR OFFICER PRESENT (SEE FLAG 66) A	B
	FEET	FEET	FEET	FEET	FEET	FEET
1	10.20	14.40	10.20	14.40	8.00	6.40
2	7.73	10.88	7.73	10.88	6.56	5.25
4	3.60	5.13	4.81	6.7[illegible]	4.90	3.90
6			3.60	5.13		

A DIAGRAM AND TABLE TO SHOW THE EXACT PROPORTION AND POSITION OF EACH FEATURE OF THE STARS AND STRIPES, ACCORDING TO THE REGULATIONS OF THE ARMY AND NAVY

17 NATIONAL STANDARD

18 CAVALRY STANDARD

19 FIELD ARTILLERY STANDARD

20 U. S. MOUNTED ENGINEERS

21 U. S. SIGNAL CORPS

22 STANDARD WAR 1812

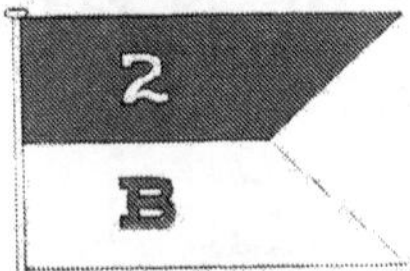

23 GUIDON—CAVALRY

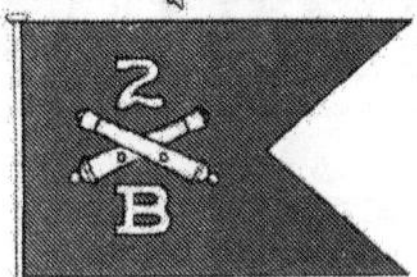

24 GUIDON FIELD ARTILLERY

25 GUIDON ENGINEERS MOUNTED COMPANY

26 GUIDON ENGINEERS MOUNTED SECTION

27 GUIDON SIGNAL CORPS

28 GUIDON AERO SQUADRON

29 GUIDON TELEGRAPH CO

30 GUIDON—MOTOR TRUCK CO

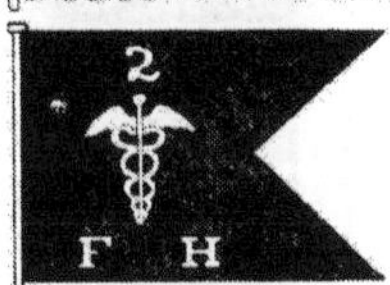

31 GUIDON FIELD HOSPITAL

32 GUIDON AMBULANCE CO.

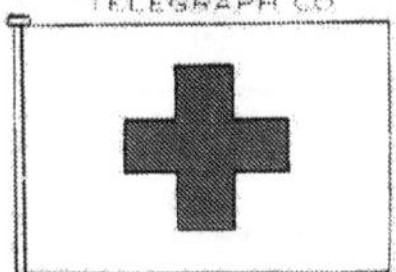
33 FIELD HOSPITAL FLAG

34 GUIDON—CIVIL WAR

35 LIEUT GENERAL BOAT & AUTO FLAG

36 MAJOR GENERAL BOAT & AUTO FLAG

37 BRIGADIER GEN BOAT & AUTO FLAG

38 CHIEF UMPIRE AUTO FLAG

39 ARTILLERY DIST COMMANDER

40 POST COMMANDER BOAT FLAG

41 AMBULANCE

42 AMMUNITION TRAIN

43 CAMP COLORS

44 CHAPLAIN

45 VESSELS TRANSPORT SERVICE

46 SUBMARINE DEFENSE VESSELS

47 ORDNANCE VESSELS

48 ENGINEER VESSELS

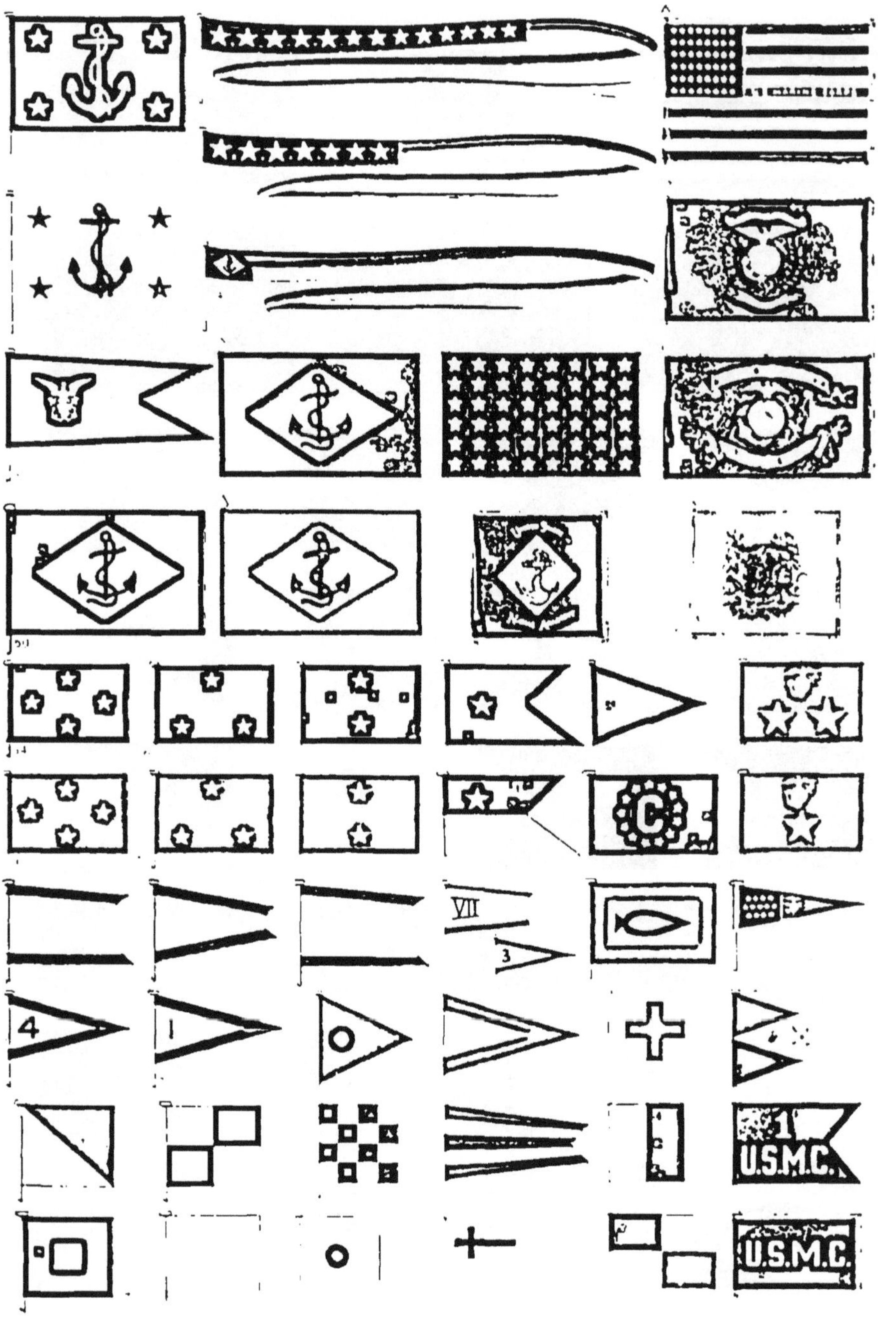
VII
3
4
1
C
1
U.S.M.C.
U.S.M.C.

teen white stars flies in the bows of the boat in which he is embarked.

75. The flag of a brigadier general of the United States Marine Corps is similar to that of a major general (69), except that it carries one star instead of two.

76. The flag of the commander of a destroyer flotilla is a swallow-tail pennant of plain white bordered above and below with blue.

77. The commander of a submarine force has a triangular swallow-tail pennant bordered above with blue and below with red.

78. The commanders of district patrol forces carry a swallow-tail pennant having a white field bordered by red above and below.

79. Section commanders of the patrol force carry a smaller duplicate of 78, with the number of the section in Roman numerals thereon.

79½. The division commander of the patrol force carries a red-bordered white triangular pennant with the number of the division in Arabic notation.

80. When submarines are operating in times of peace a submarine warning flag is flown on their tenders, while the submarine itself bears on one of its periscopes a small metal flag of the same design.

81. The boat flag of a post commander of the United States Marine Corps is a triangular pennant of blue and red, blue at the hoist and red in the fly, with thirteen white stars on the blue and the insignia of the Marine Corps on the red.

82. Destroyer division commanders carry a white triangular pennant bordered with blue, with their numbers indicated on the white field.

83. The flag of a division commander of the submarine force is a white triangle bordered with blue at the top and red below, showing the number of the division in red on the white.

84. The battle efficiency pennant is one of the most coveted trophies of the American navy. There is one for each class of ships, such as battleships, destroyers, and submarines. The ship of a given class which, during the preceding year, has shown by her practice and performance the ability to hit most often and quickest, to steam the farthest with the least expenditure of fuel, water, etc., to run longest without breakdown, and which otherwise gives evidence that she might be expected to give a better account of herself in a battle than any other vessel of her class, is awarded the privilege of flying the battle efficiency pennant during the ensuing year. There is the keenest rivalry between the competing vessels of a class, and this little red triangular flag with the black disk is prized next to victory in battle itself.

85. This flag is flown by vessels engaged in convoy duty. When ships are engaged in maneuvers or are maneuvering in compound formation, this pennant is an indication to the other vessels of the division to take bearing and distance from the ship bearing it.

86. Hospital ships fly the Red Cross flag, and under international law they are immune from attack, unless it can be shown that the ship flying it fails to respect all of the provisions of the international compact made at Geneva.

87. This is the flag under which the marine corps moves quartermaster's supplies for its men.

88. The interrogatory flag is used in signaling when one ship wants to make a signal in the interrogatory form or to announce that it does not understand a signal.

89. The preparatory flag is displayed with a signal in order that preparations may be made to execute the signal itself uniformly and simultaneously. When the signal alone is hauled down, the ships having made ready, execute the signal. It is also hoisted when the ceremony of hoisting the colors in the morning and taking it in at sunset is the next thing on the program. It is raised five minutes before the ceremony begins. Upon being hauled down by the flagship, all ships execute the colors ceremony simultaneously.

90. This flag is displayed either to countermand the last signal made or the one then being shown.

91. This pennant has two uses. Its first use is in answering a call for a semaphore or wigwag message, being hoisted half way when the ship is ready to receive the message, and all the way when the message has been completely received. It is then hauled down. Used thus, it might be said to be the "Aye, aye, sir" flag of the navy. Its other use is as a decimal or divisional flag in flags indicating numerals and quantities.

92. This is the "No" flag of the navy. It is used to negative a request, or to say "No" to a question.

93. The brigade pennant of the United States Marine Corps has a swallow-tailed blue field, with the number of the brigade and the initials of the corps in gold.

94. When a ship asks permission of the flagship to do this or that, the force commander hoists this flag with the number distinguishing the vessel making the request, as a sign that it has been granted.

95. The yellow flag, as is well known, is the one which proclaims that there is contagious disease aboard.

96. This flag has two uses. Hoisted at the main mast, it means that the vessel displaying it is engaged on dispatch duty. It is always carried in a roll at the fore mast of vessels in formation, so that it can be displayed, or "broken out," as the sailors say, instantly, to indicate an accident or derangement on board that vessel and to warn other ships to keep clear. Hoisted half way, clear of the smokestack, it indicates a man overboard.

97. The church pennant is always displayed when divine services on board are in progress.

98. The cornet flag, displayed at the yard arm, calls all vessels present to receive a semaphore or wig-wag message. Displayed at the fore mast, it is notice to all officers and men to come on board at once.

99. The guidon of the United States Marine Corps has a blue field, is gold fringed, and bears in gold on the field the initials of the corps.

100. This flag, displayed with 101, 102, 103, 104, 105, 106, 107, 108, 110, and 111, indicates that they represent in value the numerals given below them. If those flags are not displayed

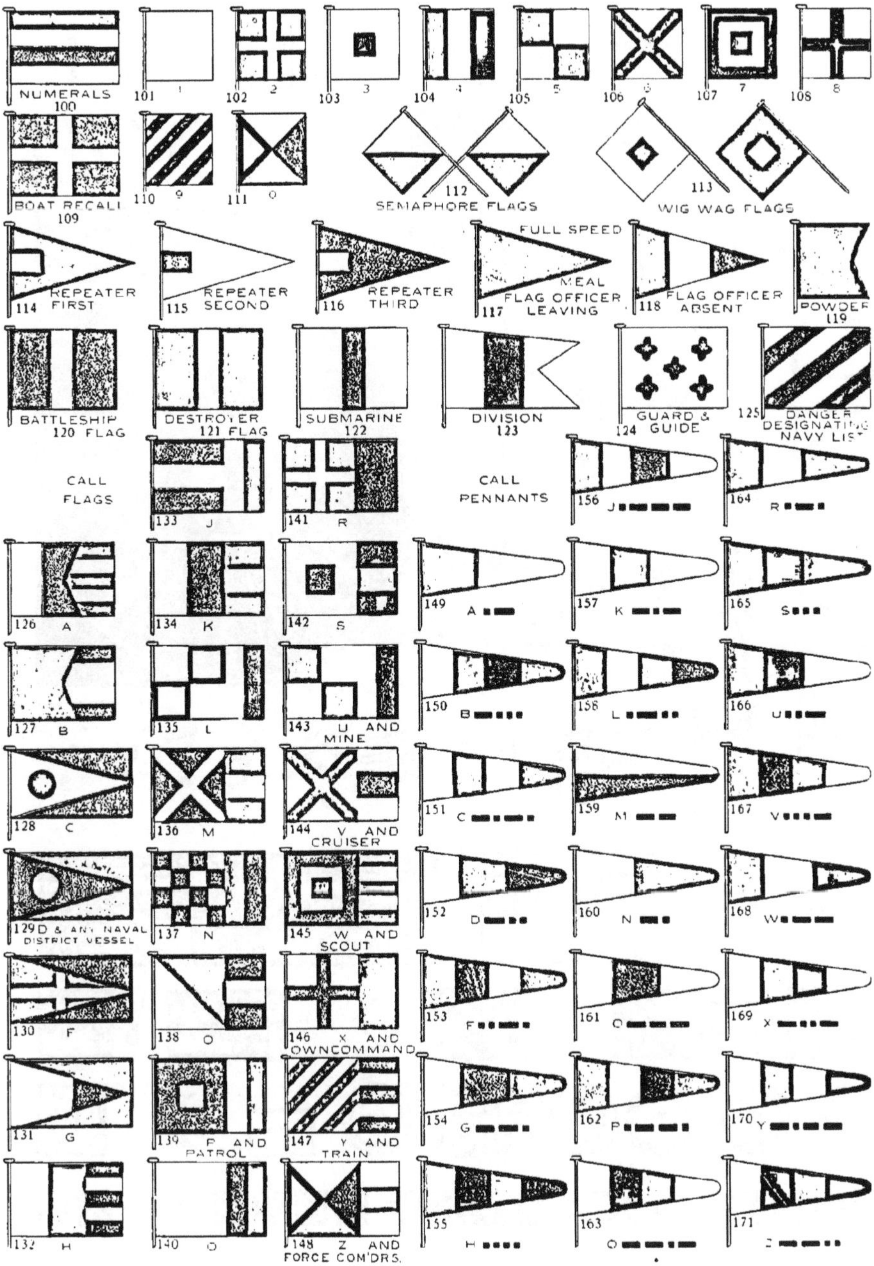
NUMERALS 100
101 1
102 2
103 3
104 4
105 5
106 6
107 7
108 8
BOAT RECALL 109
110 9
111 0
112 SEMAPHORE FLAGS
113 WIG WAG FLAGS
114 REPEATER FIRST
115 REPEATER SECOND
116 REPEATER THIRD
FULL SPEED
MEAL
117 FLAG OFFICER LEAVING
118 FLAG OFFICER ABSENT
POWDER 119
BATTLESHIP 120 FLAG
DESTROYER 121 FLAG
SUBMARINE 122
DIVISION 123
124 GUARD & GUIDE
125 DANGER DESIGNATING NAVY LIST
CALL FLAGS
CALL PENNANTS
126 A
127 B
128 C
129 D & ANY NAVAL DISTRICT VESSEL
130 F
131 G
132 H
133 J
134 K
135 L
136 M
137 N
138 O
139 P AND PATROL
140 Q
141 R
142 S
143 U AND MINE
144 V AND CRUISER
145 W AND SCOUT
146 X AND OWNCOMMAND
147 Y AND TRAIN
148 Z AND FORCE COM'DRS.
149 A
150 B
151 C
152 D
153 F
154 G
155 H
156 J
157 K
158 L
159 M
160 N
161 O
162 P
163 Q
164 R
165 S
166 U
167 V
168 W
169 X
170 Y
171 Z

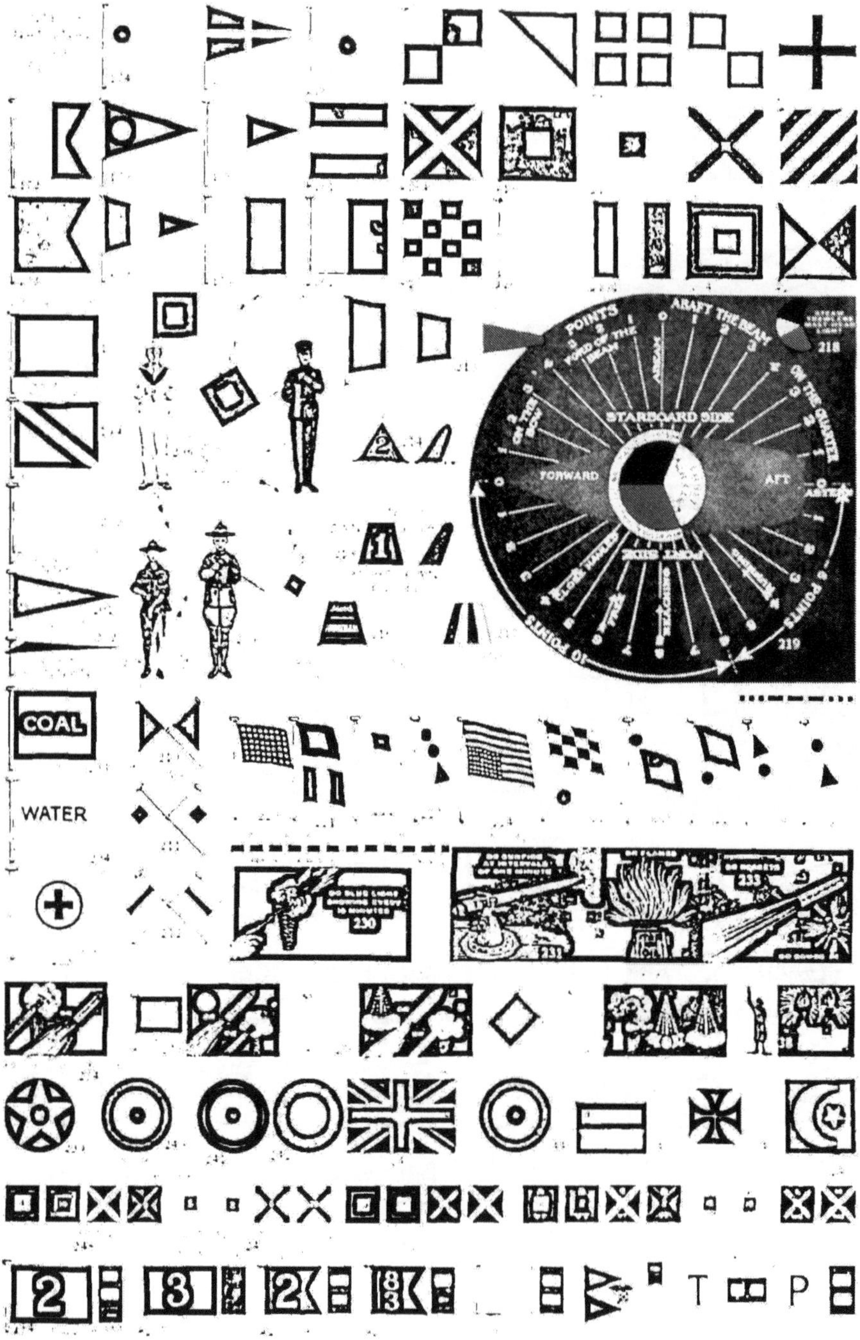
POINTS
ABAFT THE BEAM
218
ON THE QUARTER
STARBOARD SIDE
FORWARD
AFT
ASTERN
PORT SIDE
10 POINTS
219
COAL
WATER
230
231
233
T
P

or a red rocket to signify, "You are seen; assistance will be given as soon as possible" (234).

A red flag waved on shore by day, or a red light, red rocket, or red roman candle displayed by night, will signify, "Haul away" (235).

A white flag waved on shore by day, or a white light swung slowly back and forth, or a white rocket or white roman candle fired by night, will signify, "Slack away" (236).

Two flags, a white and a red, waved at the same time on shore by day, or two lights, a white and a red, slowly swung at the same time, or a blue pyrotechnic light burned by night, will signify, "Do not attempt to land in your own boats; it is impossible" (237).

A man on shore beckoning by day, or two torches burning near together by night, will signify, "This is the best place to land" (238).

Any of these signals may be answered from the vessel as follows: In the day-time, by waving a flag, a handkerchief, a hat, or even the hand; at night, by firing a rocket, a blue light, or a gun, or by showing a light over the ship's gunwale for a short time and then concealing it.

239-246. The insignia of the airplanes of the various countries are here shown. The United States makes use of the five-pointed star, Great Britain still retains her three crosses of the union jack, Germany marks hers with the Prussian black cross, and Turkey displays the familiar star and crescent.

248-253. These represent the company signal flags of the U. S. infantry and of the militia and volunteers.

254-261. Distinguishing flags and lanterns of army headquarters.

262. The flag of the Secretary of the Treasury, who is Commander-in-Chief of the Coast Guard and Public Health Service, has a blue field with crossed anchors in white centered thereon, the design surrounded by thirteen white five-pointed stars. This flag is flown when the Secretary of the Treasury is aboard vessels of the Treasury service.

263. The U. S. Coast Guard flag was adopted in 1790 for the Revenue Cutter Service, now merged with the Life Saving Service into the Coast Guard. The sixteen vertical stripes proclaim the sixteen States that were in the Union at the time the design was adopted; its red eagle, with the stars above and the escutcheon on its breast, bespeaks the Federal service. The badge on the seventh red stripe bears a shield surrounded by the motto, "Semper Paratus 1790" (Always prepared). It appears on the flag to show that it represents the Coast Guard. The same flag without the badge denotes the custom houses of the United States. In time of war the Coast Guard operates as a part of the United States Navy and then uses the flags and pennants of the naval service.

264-265. The design of the arms on the flags of the Secretary and Assistant Secretary of Commerce are identical, except for the transposition of colors. It is taken from the official seal of the department and shows on the upper part of the escutcheon a ship at full sail and on the lower part a lighthouse illumined. The service flag is hoisted at the fore mast on holidays, on occasions of official ceremonies, when entering a port after an extended voyage, and at any other time when the national ensign is hoisted. At no time should a service flag be displayed without the national ensign. These flags are shown as follows: 268, 272, 276, 280.

266. The Assistant Secretary of the Treasury has the same flag as the Secretary of the Treasury, except that the colors are transposed. His flag is never flown in the presence of the flag of his ranking officer, 262.

267. The pennant of the U. S. Coast Guard has thirteen stars and vertical red and white stripes. It was adopted in 1790, and is always displayed by Coast Guard cutters in commission. In time of war the Coast Guard operates as part of the U. S. Navy and wears the commission pennant of the navy.

268. The service flag of the Bureau of Navigation, with its white ship in a red disc on a blue ground is flown by all vessels of the Navigation Service during daylight hours.

269. The flag of the Commissioner of Navigation is blue, bearing a full-rigged ship in white in the center. It is flown on Department of Commerce vessels when the Commissioner of Navigation is on board.

270. The flag of the Customs Service is the same as that of the Coast Guard, except that the badge of the latter is omitted.

271. The jack of the Coast Guard Service is a reproduction of the canton of the ensign of the same service. The jack of the Coast Guard is used only at parades on shore. Since the national ensign has been used as the ensign of the Coast Guard, the old Coast Guard ensign is used only as a distinguishing flag, and the only jack displayed on vessels of the Coast Guard is 4.

272. A white fish on a red diamond imposed upon a blue ground constitutes the flag flown by the vessels of the Bureau of Fisheries. It was adopted in 1896.

273. The Commissioner of Fisheries has one of the newest flags in the Federal service. It is a blue banner with a white fish in the center and was adopted July 22, 1913.

274. The flag of the U. S. Public Health Service was adopted in 1894. It is the international yellow quarantine flag with the service shield thereon. The fouled anchor stands for the seamen in need of assistance, and the caduceus represents the herald or physician who is to bring restored health.

275. This is the flag of the senior officer present, and is flown in the Coast Guard to indicate that the ship which displays it bears the force commander.

276. The flag of the Bureau of Lighthouses is a white triangular pennant, red bordered, and bearing in the white field, parallel with the staff and next to it, a blue lighthouse.

277. The flag of the Commissioner of Lighthouses has the white field and blue lighthouse of the service flag placed upon a square field of blue.

278. The Surgeon General of the U. S. Public Health Service flies a flag of blue, bearing the fouled anchor, of the official shield of the service. The design is white.

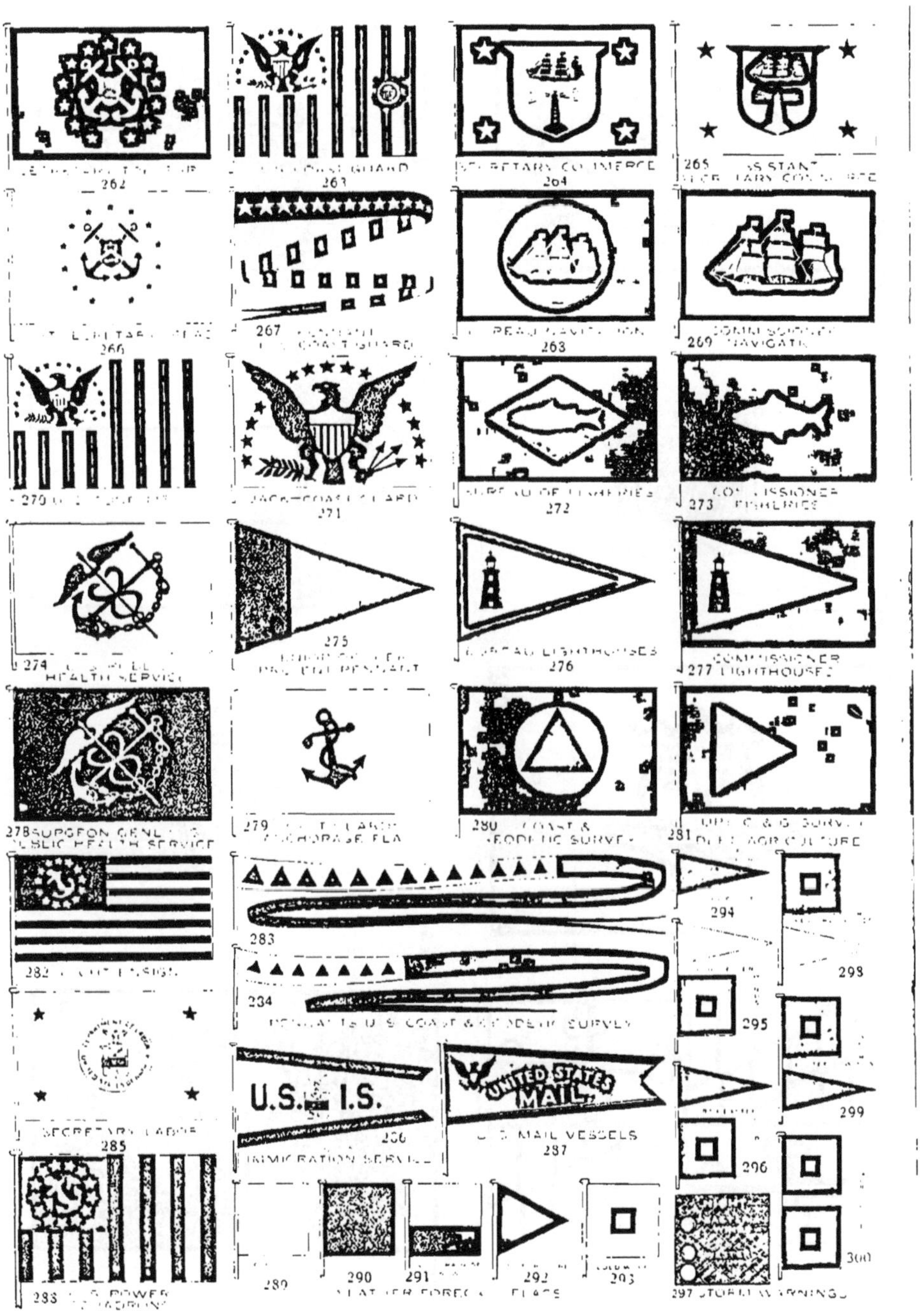

262
263
264
265
266
267
268
269
270
271
272
273
274
275
276
277
278
279
280
281
282
283
284
285
286
287
288
289
290
291
292
293
294
295
296
297
298
299
300
U.S. I.S.
UNITED STATES MAIL
U.S. MAIL VESSELS
SECRETARY LABOR

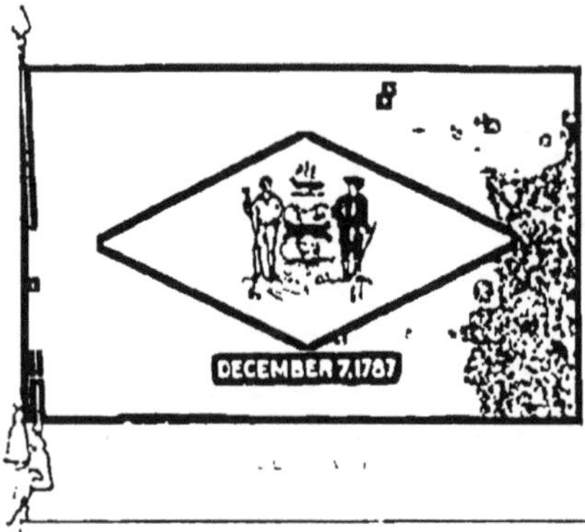
DECEMBER 7,1787

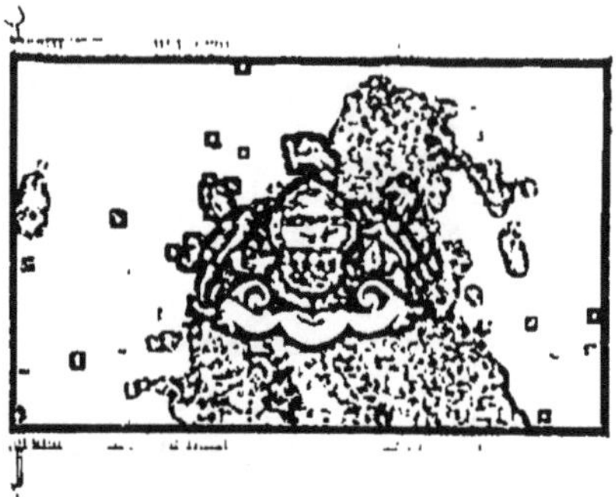

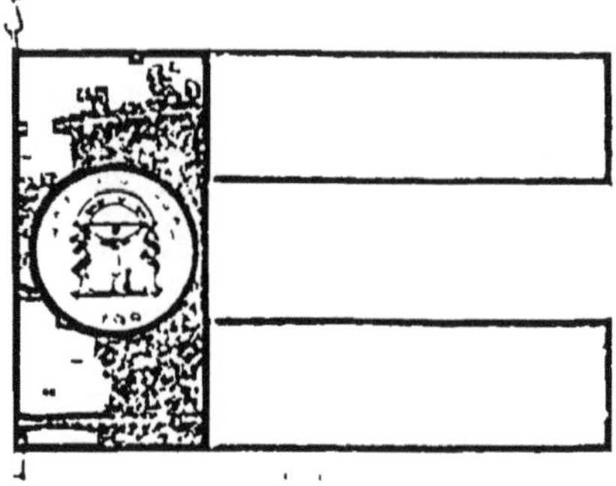

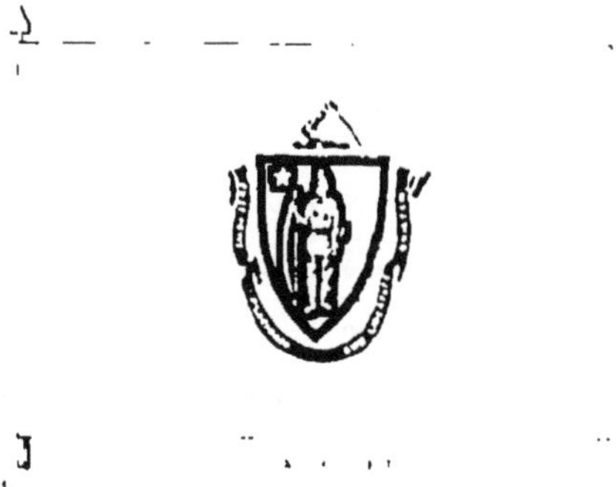

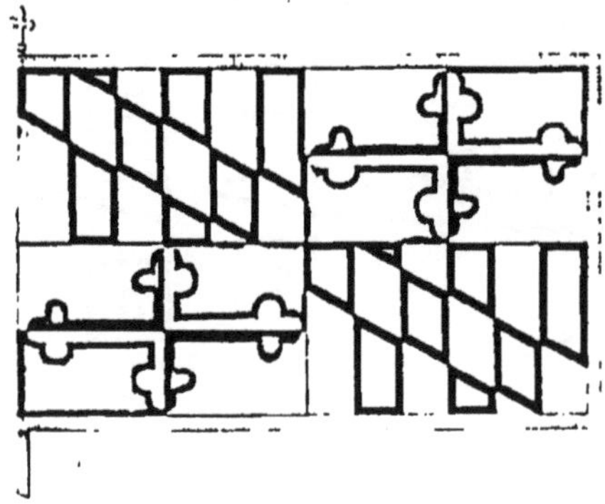

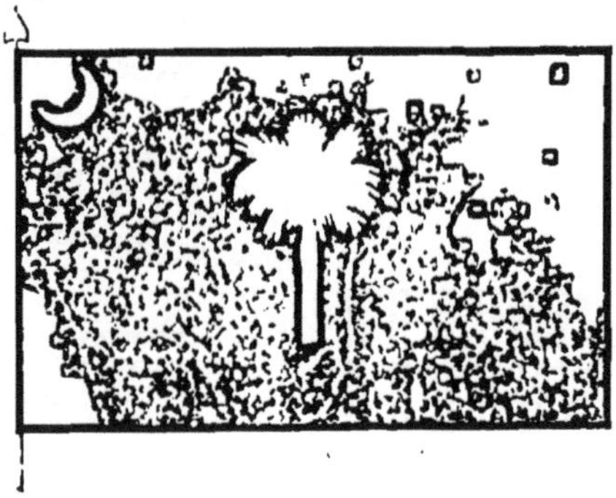

WHEN THE COMMANDER-IN-CHIEF OF THE NAVY REVIEWS THE FLEET

Photograph by [illegible]

To the left is seen the U. S. S. *Mayflower*, the presence of the President on board being indicated by his flag which flies from the main-mast. In the central foreground is an American battleship full dressed, displaying its largest ensign, its jack, and its rainbow of signal flags. The presidential salute of 21 guns is being fired by the battleship.

OUR STATE FLAGS

309 NEW HAMPSHIRE

310 VIRGINIA

311 NEW YORK

312 NORTH CAROLINA

313 RHODE ISLAND

314 VERMONT

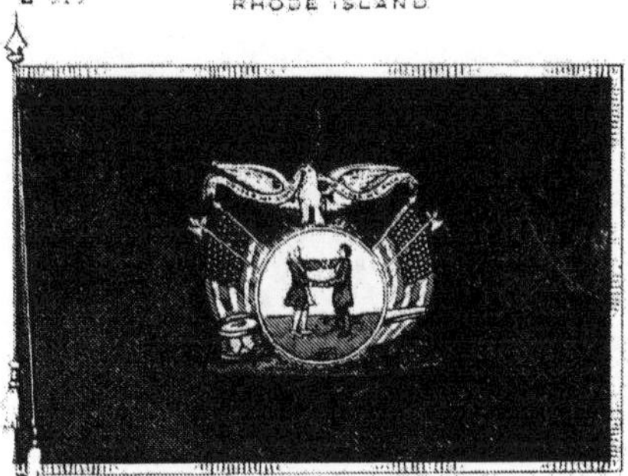

315 KENTUCKY (UNOFFICIAL)
NO STATE FLAG

316 TENNESSEE

OHIO

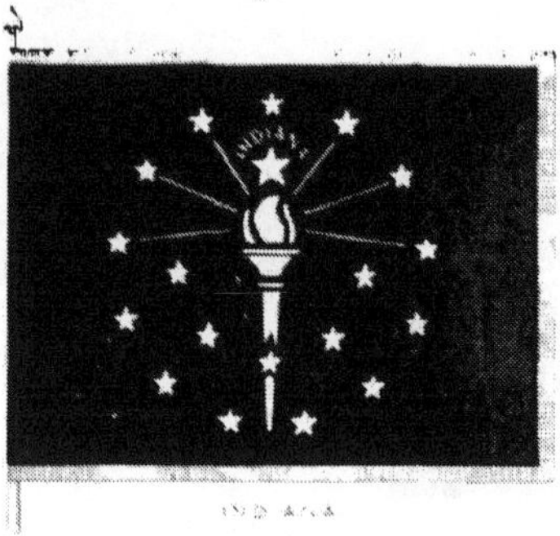

ILLINOIS

MAINE

pendicular bar appears the coat-of-arms of the State. This coat-of-arms has three pillars supporting an arch with the word "Constitution" engraved thereon. The three departments of government are supposed to be represented by the three pillars. On the pillars are engraved the words "Wisdom," "Justice," "Moderation," these words being supposed to typify the legislative, executive, and judicial branches of the State government.

305. CONNECTICUT'S colors consist of a dark blue background, bearing the State seal in the center. The seal has three grape vines, representing the three original colonies of Connecticut — Hartford, Windsor, and Wethersfield. Beneath the vines is the State motto, "Qui transtulit sustinet." The Connecticut State flag was adopted by the General Assembly in 1897. Its dimensions are five feet six inches by four feet four inches. The Latin inscription is a survival of the Nutmeg State's Colonial banner and, freely translated, means, "He who brought us over sustains us."

306. MASSACHUSETTS.—By a law approved in 1908 the flag of the Commonwealth bears on one side a representation of the coat-of-arms of the State, upon a white field, and on the other side a blue field bearing the representation of a green pine tree against a white background. When carried as colors by troops, or otherwise, the flag is bordered by a fringe and surmounted by a cord and tassels, the fringe, cord, and tassels being of golden yellow. The staff is of white ash or wood of similar light color, tipped with a spearhead of gilt. The coat-of-arms was authorized under a law of 1885. It consists of a shield having a blue field, with an Indian man, dressed in shirt, hunting breeches, and moccasins, holding in his right hand a bow and in his left hand an arrow pointing downward, all of gold; in the upper corner of the field above his right arm is a silver star with five points. The crest is a wreath of blue and gold, whereon, in gold, is a right arm, bent at the elbow, clothed and ruffled, with the hand grasping a broad sword. The motto is "Ense petit placidam sub libertate quietem."

307. MARYLAND.—One of the oldest flags in the world at the date of its official adoption, the State flag of Maryland is unique in design and striking in its history. Although it was the flag of the proprietary government of Maryland generations before American independence was dreamed of, and has continued in use from that day to this, it was not officially adopted until 1904. It represents the escutcheon of the paternal coat-of-arms of Lord Baltimore. After reciting that it is eminently fitting that, by reason of its historic interest and meaning, as well as for its beauty and harmony of colors, the flag adopted should be one which from the earliest settlement of the province to the present time has been known and distinguished as the flag of Maryland, the resolutions then provide that the first and fourth quarters consist of six vertical bars, alternately gold and black, with a diagonal band on which the colors are reversed; the second and third quarters consist of a quartered field of red and white, charged with a Greek cross, its arms terminating in trefoils, with the colors transposed, red being on the white ground and white on the red, and all being represented as on the escutcheon of the present great seal of Maryland. The flag always is to be so arranged upon the staff as to have the black stripes on the diagonal band of the first quarter at the top of the staff. It is to be displayed from the State House at Annapolis continually during the session of the General Assembly and on such other public occasions as the Governor of the State shall order and direct.

308. SOUTH CAROLINA'S flag is reminiscent of secession times. Following that State's withdrawal from the Union, its legislature decided that it was a separate nation and should have a national banner. A resolution was therefore adopted in 1861 providing that "the national flag or ensign of South Carolina should be blue, with a golden palmetto upright upon a white oval in the center thereof, and a white crescent in the upper flagstaff corner of the flag." Two days later a resolution was adopted by the two houses providing that the white medallion and golden palmetto be dispensed with and in their place a white palmetto inserted. From that time to this South Carolina has had a blue flag, with the white crescent and the white palmetto. When the State entered the Confederate Union its national flag became the State flag, and continues such to this day. In 1910 a law was made providing that State flags should be manufactured in the textile department of Clemson College and sold at approximate cost to the people. Another provision is that the State flag shall be displayed daily, except in rainy weather, from the staff of the State House and every court house, one building of the State University, and of each State college, and upon every public-school building except during vacation. Any person who maltreats or desecrates a flag of the State, wherever displayed, shall be guilty of a misdemeanor, and upon conviction punished by a fine of not more than a hundred dollars or imprisonment for not more than thirty days.

309. NEW HAMPSHIRE had no State flag authorized and described by law until 1909. In that year an act was adopted providing that the flag should be blue, bearing upon its center in suitable proportions and colors a representation of the State seal. The inscription is as follows: "Sigillum Republicæ Neo Hantoniesis 1784" (Seal of the Commonwealth of New Hampshire). The shield is surrounded by a wreath of laurel leaves with nine stars interspersed. When used for military purposes, the flag is to conform to the regulations of the United States. Under this law New Hampshire's flag is to be displayed above the State House whenever the legislature is in session, and during meetings of the Governor and council when expedient, and upon such other occasions as the Governor may designate. During the Civil War, New Hampshire regiments carried yellow-fringed white flags, with blue and white cords and tassels, bearing on one side the State coat-of-arms and on the other that of the United States.

310. VIRGINIA'S flag is of blue bunting, sixteen by twenty feet, with a circular white ground in the center, in which the seal of the

325 ARKANSAS

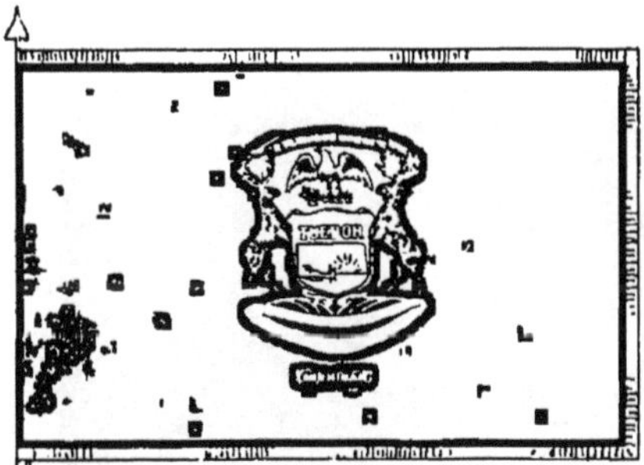

326 MICHIGAN

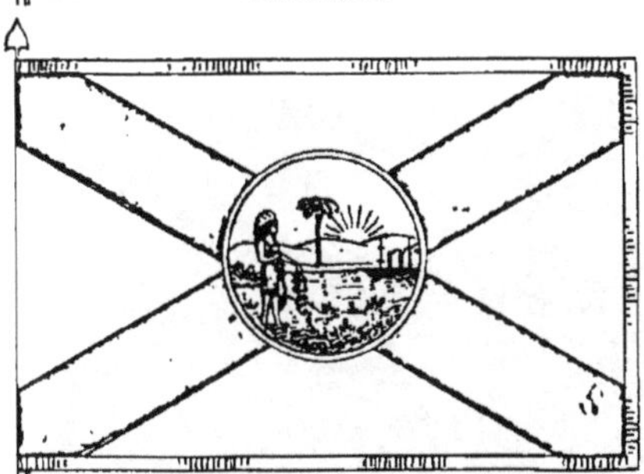

327 FLORIDA

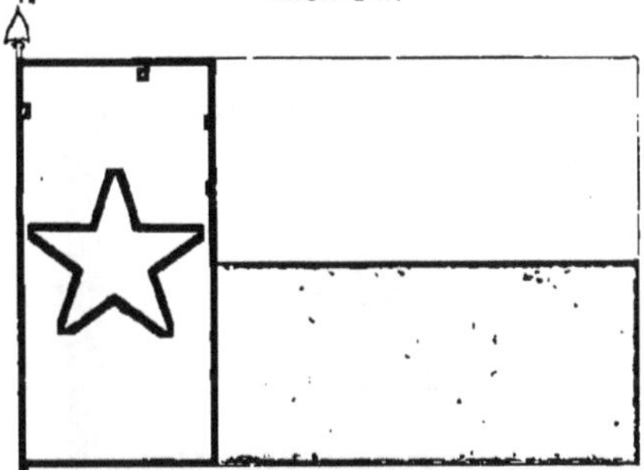

328 TEXAS

329 IOWA

330 WISCONSIN

331 CALIFORNIA

332 MINNESOTA

OREGON

KANSAS

WEST VIRGINIA

NEVADA

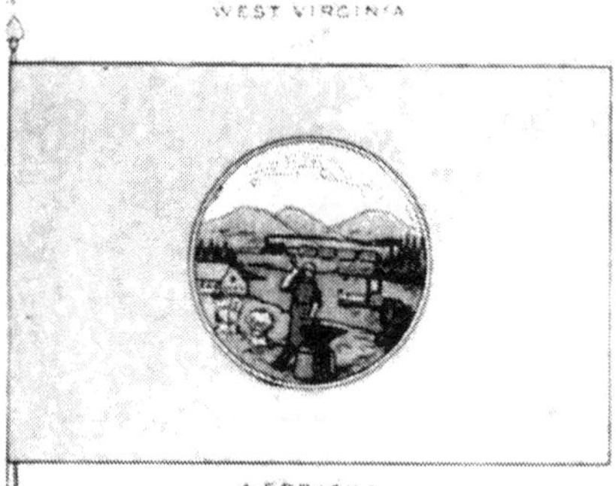

NEBRASKA

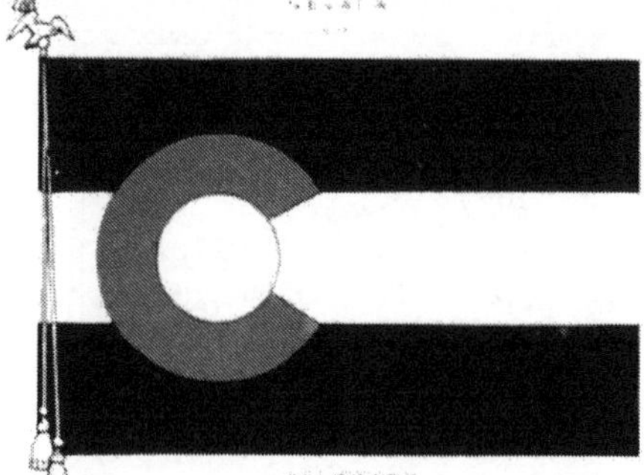

COLORADO

NORTH DAKOTA

SOUTH DAKOTA

by an eagle bearing in its beak a streamer carrying the legend "United We Stand, Divided We Fall." It is said that the original intention of the seal was to represent two friends in hunter's garb, their right hands clasped, their left resting on each other's shoulders, their feet on the verge of a precipice, which gave significance to the legend. But the engravers for the State have uniformly dressed the figures more to suit their ideals, with varying heraldic effect. The escutcheon is supported by four United States flags, a drum and a cannon.

316. TENNESSEE.—This unique flag was adopted in 1905. It consists of a flag one and two-thirds times as long as it is wide. At the outer or free end is a blue bar separated from the red field by a thin white stripe. Superimposed upon the red field is a circular disk of blue separated from the field by a thin circle of white, its width the same as the width of the white stripe separating the blue bar from the red field. Upon the blue of the circular disk are arranged three five-pointed stars of white distributed at equal intervals around a point which is the center of the blue field. Tennessee was the third State to join the Union (after the original thirteen), a fact which the three stars recall.

317. OHIO has the only pennant-shaped flag among all the States. The law making it the official ensign of the "Buckeye State" was adopted in 1902. The outer quarter of the field is swallow-tailed, the field itself consisting of five stripes—three red and two white—red at the bottom and top. At the staff end of the field is a triangular blue canton with the base resting on the staff and the apex reaching half way across the field. On this canton is a large circular "O" in white, inside of which is a red disk. Seventeen stars, representing all of the States at the time of Ohio's entrance into the Union, are grouped around the circular "O." All of these stars are five-pointed.

318. LOUISIANA.—Those who contend that the Stars and Stripes were used unofficially long before they were adopted by the Continental Congress on June 14, 1777, can point to the history of the Louisiana State flag as showing that banners are often used unofficially long before being officially adopted. It is said that this flag is a hundred years old, having become the unofficial flag of Louisiana about the time of the War of 1812, yet it was not legally adopted until July 1, 1912. The measure changing it to the flag of the State is simply a statute of identification, and sets forth that it shall consist of a solid blue field with the coat-of-arms of the State, a pelican feeding its young, in white in the center, with a ribbon beneath, also in white, containing in blue the motto of the State, "Union, Justice, Confidence." The law provides that the flag shall be displayed on the State House whenever the General Assembly is in session, and on public buildings throughout the State on all regular holidays, and whenever otherwise directed by the Governor or the General Assembly.

319. INDIANA.—Although the legislature of the State of Indiana declared in 1901 that its emblem should be no other than the American flag itself, it reconsidered this action in 1917 and adopted a State emblem. The field of the flag is blue; its dimensions are five feet six inches fly by four feet four inches on the staff, and upon the field is centered a flaming torch in gold, or buff, with nineteen stars. Thirteen stars are circled around the torch, representing the original thirteen States. Inside this circle is a half circle of five stars below the torch, representing the five States admitted to the Union prior to Indiana. The outer circle of stars is so arranged that one of them appears directly in the middle at the top of the circle. The word "Indiana" is placed in a half circle over a large star typifying the State, which is situated just above the flame of the torch. Rays from the torch radiate to the three stars of the outer circle. This banner is to be carried in addition to the American flag by the military forces of Indiana and in all public functions in which the State officially appears.

320. MISSISSIPPI is one of the States that have had more than one flag. The old flag was white, with a blue canton with a single white star thereon. On the body of the white was a green tree. The flag was fringed with red and the pike was surmounted by a tomahawk. After the Civil War the State adopted a new flag. This consists of a blue, white and red field, the red at the bottom, with a red canton reaching down to the red stripe of the field. A St. Andrew's cross with thirteen stars is imposed upon the canton. The tomahawk of the old flagstaff is replaced on the new pike by a regulation spear head.

321. ILLINOIS' State flag was authorized in the year 1915. The law provides that the reproduction of the emblem on the great seal of Illinois be permitted when reproduced in black or in natural colors on a white background for use as a State banner. The seal of the State of Illinois was adopted in 1819, the year after the State was admitted to the Union. In the center is an American eagle perched on an American shield. Back of the shield and helping to support it is an olive branch. In its beak the eagle holds a scroll containing the motto "State Sovereignty—National Union."

322. ALABAMA's colors were adopted by the act of February 16, 1895, which provides that the flag of the State shall be a crimson cross of St. Andrew upon a field of white. The bars forming the cross shall be not less than six inches broad, and must extend diagonally across the flag from side to side. The flag shall be hoisted on the dome of the capitol when the two houses of the legislature are in session, and shall be used by the State on all occasions when it may be necessary or consistent to display a flag, except when in the opinion of the Governor the national flag should be displayed. It is said that the purpose of the legislature in enacting the State flag law was to preserve in permanent form some of the more distinctive features of the Confederate battle flag, especially the St. Andrew's cross (see 375). This being true, the Alabama flag should be square in all its lines and measurements and conform to the well-known battle flag of the Confederacy.

MONTANA
341

WASHINGTON (UNOFFICIAL)
342

IDAHO
343

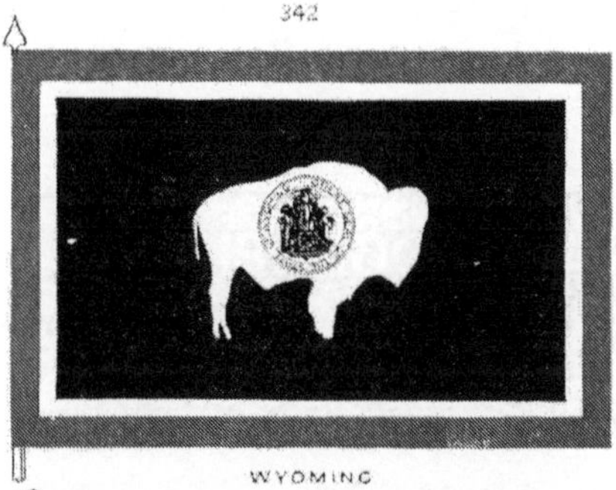

WYOMING
344

UTAH
345

OKLAHOMA
346

NEW MEXICO
347

ARIZONA
348

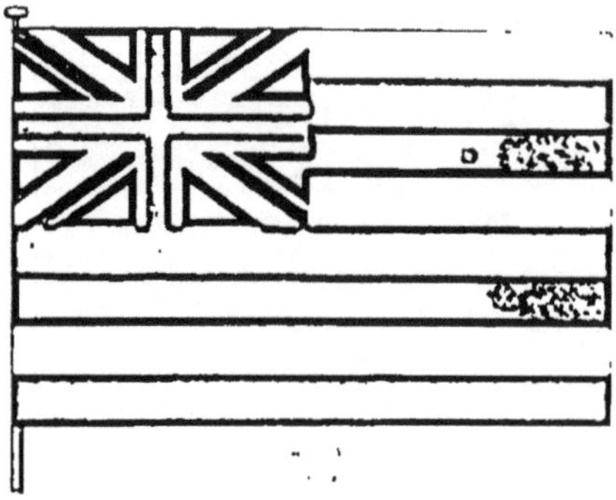

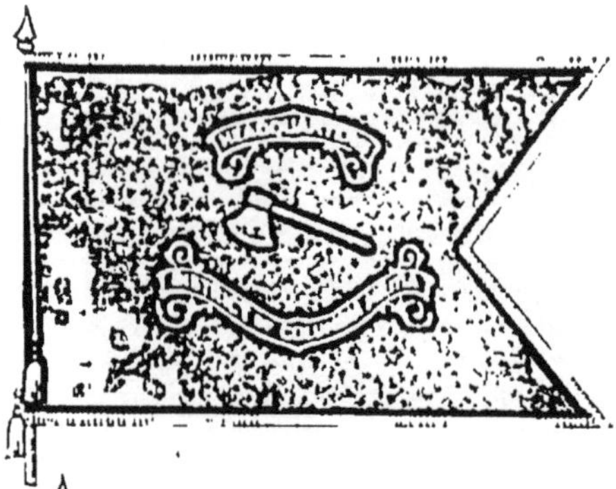

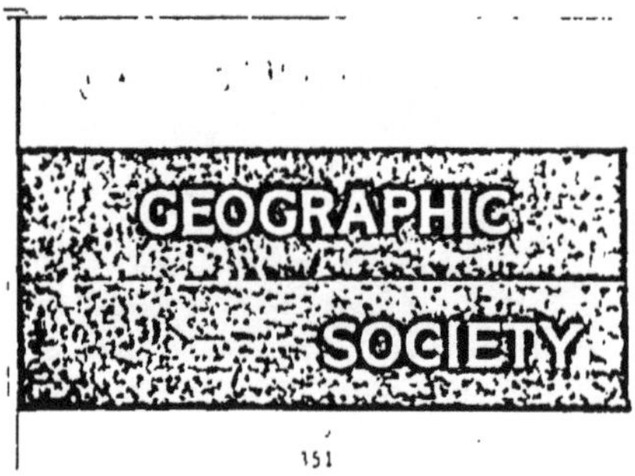

351

SEAL ALASKA
353

PHILIPPINE ISLANDS
354

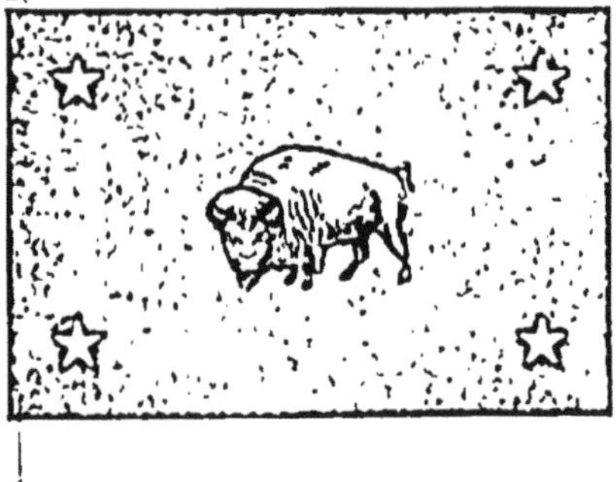

330 WISCONSIN'S State flag was officially adopted in 1913. The law provides that it shall be of dark blue silk, five feet six inches fly and four feet four inches on the pike; the State coat-of-arms is embroidered on each side in silk of appropriate color and design, and the edges of the flag are trimmed with knotted fringe of yellow silk two and one-half inches wide. The pike is nine feet long, including the spearhead and ferrule; the cord eight feet six inches long, with two tassels composed of blue and white silk strands intermixed. Service flags may be of bunting or other material of such size as may be required, and the coat-of-arms may be represented otherwise than by embroidery.

331 CALIFORNIA in 1911 adopted what is popularly known in the State's history as the "Bear Flag," as the official ensign of the Golden Gate Commonwealth. The law provides that the Bear Flag shall consist of a white field with a red stripe at the bottom one-sixth as wide as the field. In the upper left-hand corner of the field is a single red star, and at the bottom of the white field the words "California Republic." Above these words appears a California grizzly bear upon a grass plot in the position of walking toward the left of the field. The bear is dark brown in color and in length equal to one-third the length of the flag. The Bear Flag dates from the days of the California pioneers and commemorates the biggest bear known to science, the California grizzly, now extinct.

332 MINNESOTA adopted her State flag at the same time that she provided for a State flower. The ground is of white silk and the reverse side of blue silk, bordered with bullion fringe. In the center is the State seal wreathed with white moccasin flowers and a blue ground. The red ribbon of the seal bearing the motto "L'Etoile du Nord" (Star of the North) is continued through the wreath, entwining the blossoms and fluttering over the lower portion of the flag. The seal bears in gold 1819 and 1893, the dates respectively of settlement and of the adoption of the flag; also in variegated gold is the date 1858, the time of the admission of Minnesota into the Union. Below in gold letters is wrought "Minnesota." Grouped around the seal are nineteen stars, so arranged that they appear to form the points of a five-pointed star, of which the seal itself is the central portion. Four of the points are made up of four stars each; the fifth point, at the top, is made up of three stars, one of them larger than the others, typifying the North Star and representing the "North Star State." The choice of the number nineteen was made because Minnesota was the nineteenth State, after the original thirteen, admitted to the Union. The standard of the flag is surmounted by a gold gopher and tied with a gold cord and tassel.

333 OREGON followed the example of a majority of her sister States in devising her flag by making the field blue with a fringe of gold. The size of the flag is five feet six inches fly and four feet four inches on pike. The yellow fringe is four inches deep and the cord and tassel are blue and white silk intermixed. The length of the pike is ten feet, including the spearhead. The arms of the State are embroidered or painted in the center, with the number and arm of the service of the regiment underneath where it is used as a regimental flag. The arms consist of an inscription supported by 32 stars, the number of States in the Union at the time Oregon was admitted, and divided by an ordinary with the inscription "The Union." Above this inscription is an elk with branching antlers, a wagon, Pacific Ocean, a British man-of-war departing, and an American steamer arriving. Below the inscription is a sheaf, a plow, and a pick-axe. The national shield forms the crest. The figures 1859 proclaim the date of the admission of Oregon into the Union.

334 KANSAS is another State which, according to the most careful research, has not officially adopted a flag. The military officials therefore have provided a blue flag upon which is centered the coat-of-arms of the State. Agriculture is represented by the plowman in the foreground, commerce by the river and steamboat in the background. Above the plowman is a wagon train westward bound, following the course of empire. A herd of buffalo is seen retreating, pursued by two Indians on horseback. Around the top is the motto "Ad astra per aspera" (To the stars through difficulties). Underneath the motto is a cluster of thirty-four stars, representing the States in the Union at the time of the admission of Kansas.

335 WEST VIRGINIA.—The St. Louis World's Fair was responsible for the adoption of West Virginia's State flag. The West Virginia State Commission at that exposition found it necessary to adopt a flag and special design to distinguish West Virginia from other States of the Union represented. The commission at first undertook the task of designing a flag itself. The following year the legislature adopted its design, amending it only by the addition of a fringe or border of gold or orange. The law provides that the proportions of the flag shall be the same as those of the United States banner; that the field shall be pure white, upon the center of which on the obverse side shall be the great seal or coat-of-arms of the State, with the motto "Montani Semper Liberi" (Mountaineers always freemen), and beneath that, on a scroll, the legend "State of West Virginia." On the reverse side of the flag appears a sprig or sprigs of rhododendron maximum, or big laurel, the State flower, having blossoms and leaves. The field of pure white is bordered by a strip of blue, and this in turn by a strip or fringe of old gold. The flag of the State is to be employed on all occasions when a special display of the State's individuality shall become necessary or be regarded as appropriate.

336 NEVADA has had several State flags, but the one now in force dates from 1915. The flag it authorizes consists of a blue field, in the center of which is placed the great seal of the State of Nevada as designed in 1912. The seal is given a scroll border, and the words "The Great Seal of the State of Nevada" are omitted. Immediately above the seal is the word "Nevada" in silver-colored block Roman capital letters. Immediately below the seal and in the form of a semicircle are

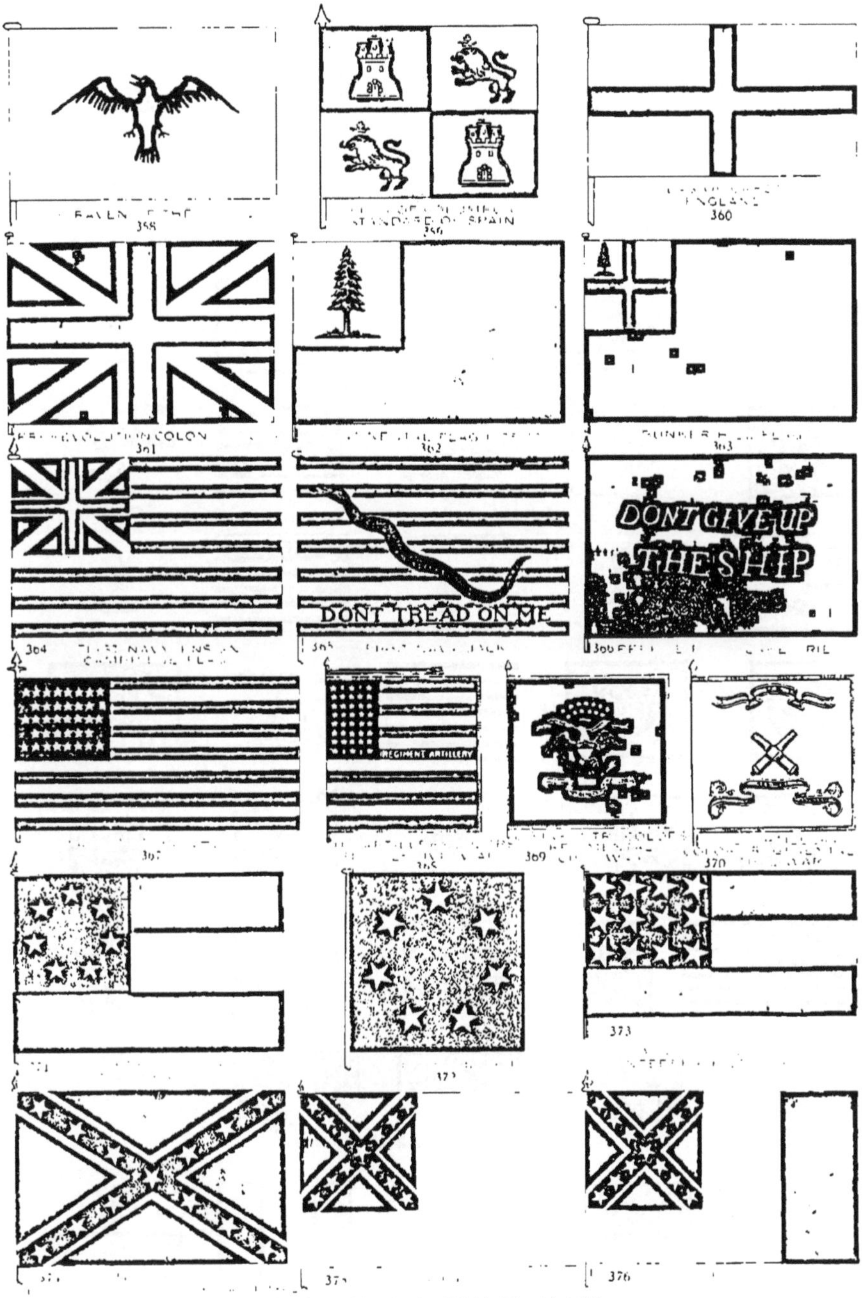

ENGLAND
360
362
363
364
DONT TREAD ON ME
DONT GIVE UP THE SHIP
REGIMENT ARTILLERY
369
370
373
376

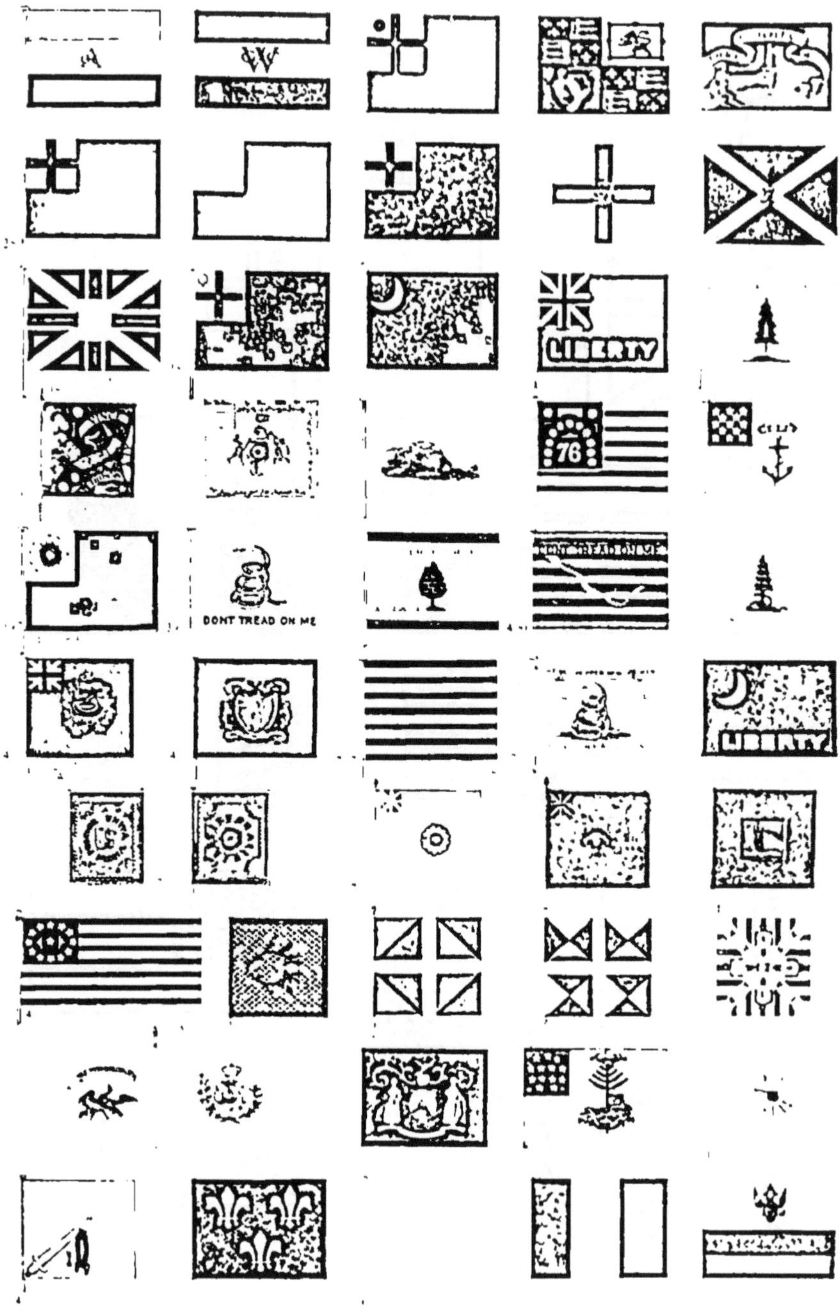
LIBERTY
76
DONT TREAD ON ME
LIBERTY

which is one fifth that of the blue field. On the obverse of the banner appears the great shield of the State of Wyoming in blue. The diameter of the shield is one-fifth the length of the flag. Attached to the flag is a cord of gold with gold tassels. All penalties provided by the laws of the State for the misuse of the national flag are applicable to the State flag.

345 Utah's flag, consisting of a blue field with a border of gold and a design in the center, was adopted in 1911. The design was revised in 1913. It consists now of a device in natural colors, the fundamental portion of which is a shield surmounted by an eagle with outstretched wings. The shield bears a beehive, on each side of which grow sego lilies, and above which is the word "Industry." At the bottom of the shield is a green field bearing the date 1847, with the word "Utah" above it. Two American flags on flagstaffs placed crosswise are so draped that they project beyond each side of the shield, the heads of the flagstaffs in front of the eagle's wings, and the bottom of each staff appearing over the face of the draped flag below the shield. Below the shield and flags and upon the blue field is the date "1896," the year in which the State was admitted to the Union. Around the entire design is a narrow circle of gold.

346 Oklahoma.—The law under which Oklahoma adopted an official State flag was enacted in 1911. The flag adopted under it consists of a red field, in the center of which is a five-pointed star of white, edged with blue, with the figures "46" in blue in the middle of the star. This number proclaims the fact that Oklahoma was the forty-sixth State to become a part of the Union. The Oklahoma flag departs from the usual in its pike head. Instead of the regulation spearhead, an eagle at rest, facing the direction of the fly, stands guard over the colors.

347 New Mexico.—Embodying elements unique in flag design, the official flag of the State of New Mexico was adopted shortly after the Commonwealth became a member of the Union. The banner has a turquoise-blue field, emblematic of the blue skies of New Mexico. It has a canton consisting of the flag of the United States in miniature in the upper left-hand corner, designating the loyalty of the people of the State to the Union; in the upper right-hand corner of the field a figure 47, the forty-seventh star and State in the American Union; in the lower right-hand corner is the great seal of the State, and upon the field running from the lower left to the upper right-hand corner are the words "New Mexico" in white. When the flag law was passed it was ordered that the embroidered banner attached to the bill should be deposited with the Secretary of State, to be faithfully kept by him in the archives of the Commonwealth.

348 Arizona.—A bill making the flag of the battleship *Arizona* the banner of the Commonwealth for which it is named failed to pass the State Senate in 1915, but a similar bill was adopted early in 1917. As legally described, the upper part of the flag consists of thirteen segments or rays, alternate red and yellow. The lower part is a solid field of blue, while upon the center is imposed a copper star. It was objected at the time of the adoption of this design that it contained nothing characteristic of Arizona, that it infringed upon the ensign of Japan, and that the effect of a star against a rising sun was a severe straining of astronomy. A substitute bill was prepared and offered to the upper house of the legislature, but the original form became a law, thus establishing one of the most striking of the State banners.

349 The flag of Hawaii preserves the crosses of St. Andrew, St. George, and St. Patrick, and carries eight stripes. Some of the Southern States retain the cross of St. Andrew, but Hawaii is the only American soil over which float the three crosses which were the cantonal feature of the first flag of the United Colonies of America (see 399).

350 The flag of the National Guard of the District of Columbia has a rectangular field, the fly end of which is swallow-tailed. Centered thereon is a small hatchet, whose alleged manipulation in connection with an apocryphal cherry tree is reputed to have put the Father of His Country to a very trying test in the matter of veracity. The designations of the forces appear on scrolls above and below the hatchet.

351 The banner of the National Geographic Society is a flag of adventure and conquest: a flag of adventure because it is ever carried beyond the horizon of known scientific fact in the hope that there may be found some new truth that will make mankind freer in the solution of the problems that ever confront it; the flag of conquest because it has gone to the tops of high mountains, to the innermost recesses of regions unexplored by civilized man, to the craters of volcanoes whose fiery depths have never been surveyed by the human eye. Those who have had its support have conquered polar ice and polar seas, have mastered many of the secrets of glacial action, have lent a hand to the solution of the great problem of vulcanism, have unearthed the holy city of the Incas, have rescued venerable trees of California from the only enemy they ever feared—the man with the ax and the saw. Its colors typifying earth, sea, and sky, proclaim the illimitable reaches of the fields of interest over which it flies, and the vastness of the work of exploration and diffusion of knowledge in which it has played no small part, and to which its future efforts shall ever be dedicated.

352 The Governor of the Panama Canal Zone flies a rectangular flag, upon which is centered the seal of the Canal Zone. This consists of an escutcheon which shows a ship under full sail passing through Gaillard Cut at the point where it divides Gold Hill and Contractors Hill. Below the escutcheon is a streamer bearing the now familiar words, "The land divided, the world united." The escutcheon and streamer are grounded upon a circle of white.

353 The seal of the Territory of Alaska is a circular field bearing in the background a sun rising over snow-capped, embattled mountains. In the right foreground are the waters that wash the shore of the territory, bearing two sailing vessels. To the left is a pier

FLAGS FAMOUS IN AMERICAN HISTORY

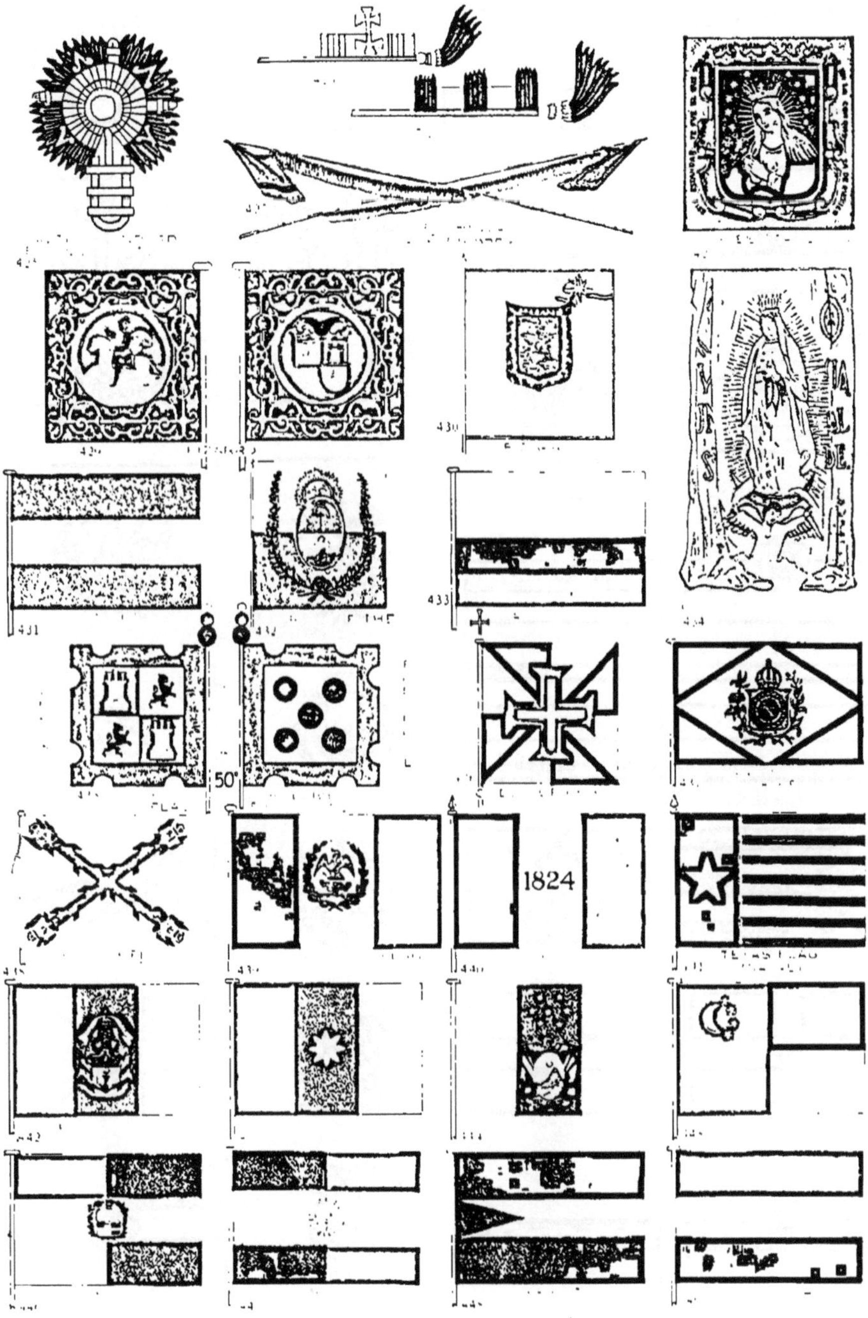
1824
TEXAS FLAG
50°

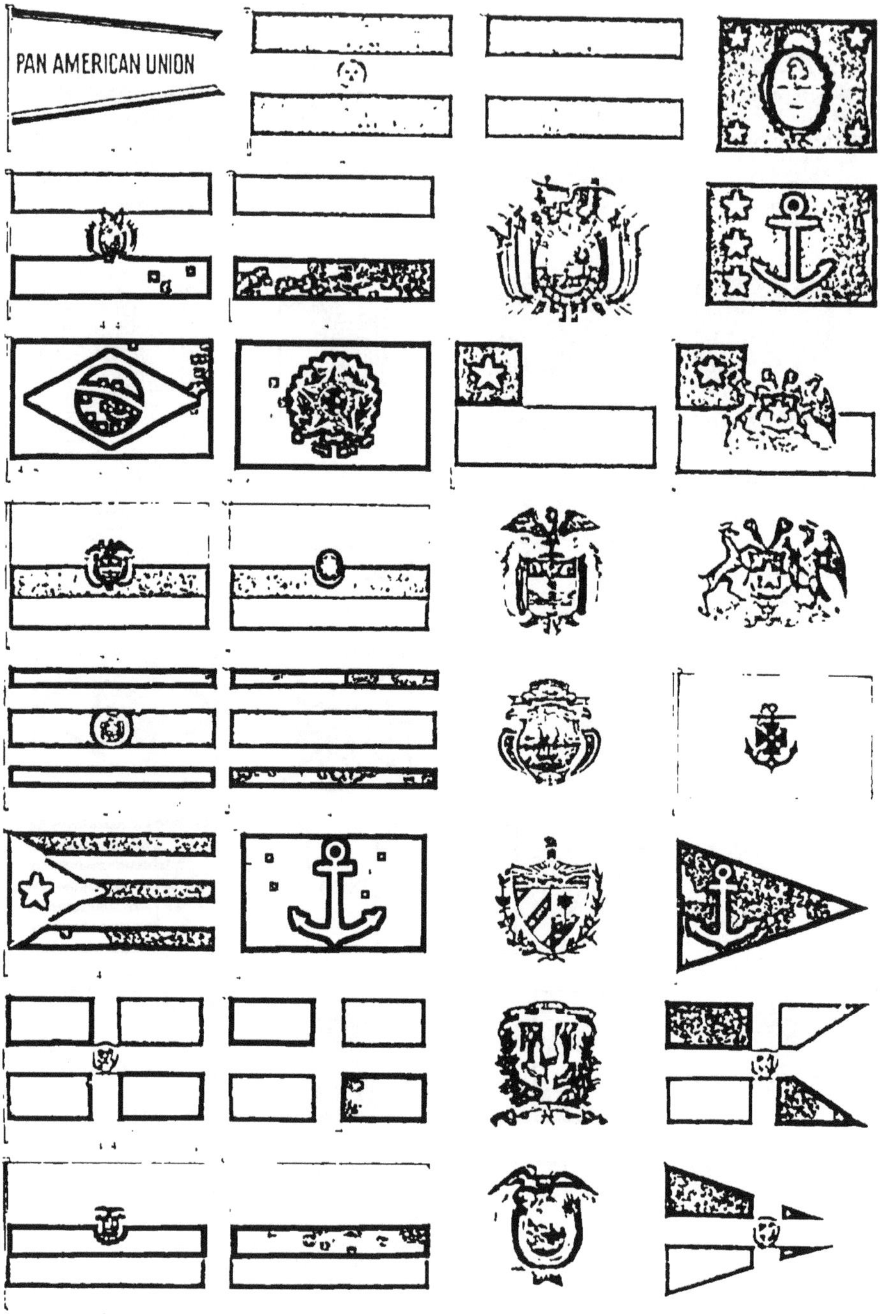
PAN AMERICAN UNION

sign of union flag). After the union of parliaments in 1707 this was the only flag officially used on land over forts and public buildings in the English colonies. With the addition of designating numerals above a small crown at the intersection of the crosses, it became the "King's Colors" for regimental troops.

362-363. CONTINENTAL AND BUNKER HILL.—The illustrations show two replicas in Annapolis of flags said to have been carried at Bunker Hill. The Trumbull painting of the battle of Bunker Hill shows 362, while others show 363. 362 was probably formed from the English ensign, shown in 1123 (in use prior to 1705), by omitting St. George's cross and substituting the pine tree, which was the symbol of the Massachusetts Bay Colony (see also 301, 302, and 401). 363 was made by inserting a pine tree in the upper left quarter of the old blue English ensign's canton (1125).

364. This was the flag hoisted by John Paul Jones on December 3, 1775, as the navy ensign of the thirteen colonies, when Commodore Esek Hopkins assumed command of the navy built by Congress. It was also hoisted by General Washington January 2, 1776, as the standard of the Continental Army and remained as our national flag until the adoption of the Stars and Stripes, June 14, 1777 (see history of "Stars and Stripes" elsewhere in this number).

365. OUR FIRST NAVY JACK.—Hoisted December 3, 1775, the same day that John Paul Jones hoisted 364 as the ensign of our new navy and that 308 was raised at the main mast as the flag of the Commander-in-Chief, Esek Hopkins (see 308 and 400).

366. PERRY'S FLAG, LAKE ERIE.—At the battle of Lake Erie, September 10, 1813, Oliver Hazard Perry, who was in command of a fleet which he had been forced to construct in feverish haste from virgin timber, unfurled from his masthead this challenge to sturdy Americanism — the dying words of brave Captain Lawrence. Under its inspiration the men fought gallantly through one of the most notable naval engagements of the war, enabling Perry at its close to send the famous message to General Harrison, "We have met the enemy and they are ours—two ships, two brigs, one schooner, and one sloop."

367. Although so distinguished a citizen as S. F. B. Morse proposed at the outbreak of the Civil War that the national flag, the Stars and Stripes, should be cut in twain, the North retaining the upper six and one-half stripes and those stars above a diagonal line extending from the head of the staff to the lower corner of the canton, while the South should be given the lower six and a half stripes and the stars below the diagonal line on the canton, the remainder of each flag being white, neither the North nor the South saw fit to follow such a suggestion. The Stars and Stripes carried by the armies of the North during the last years of the Civil War had thirty-six stars in the union, as shown in 367. When Lincoln became President, however, there were only thirty-four States, which were impersonated at the inaugural ceremonies by thirty-four little girls, who rode in a gaily decorated car in the procession and sang to the new President, "Hail, Columbia."

368. The artillery during the Civil War carried a standard with thirty-six stars arranged three stars at the top, three at the bottom, and a lay-out of thirty in six horizontal lines of five stars each. It will be noticed that this flag, like 367, was adopted after West Virginia and Nevada had entered the Union.

369. The design on the colors of infantry regiments during the Civil War was almost a counterpart of that borne on the standard of the War of 1812 (see 22). It shows an eagle displayed and bearing upon its breast a shield, with a scroll in its beak and another below it, upon which appeared the designation of each regiment. Above the eagle are thirteen golden stars arranged in two arcs.

370. The regimental colors of the United States artillery during the Civil War were yellow. Upon the field were centered two crossed cannons with a scroll above and below bearing the designation of the regiment.

371. This flag is the familiar "Stars and Bars" of the Southern Confederacy and was used from March, 1861, to May, 1863.

372. This jack of the Confederate States was made to correspond with the provisional flag of the Confederacy, known as the Stars and Bars. It probably was flown by ships of the seceding States until 1863, when the navy jack (374) was prescribed by the Secretary of the Confederate Navy.

373. This ensign was probably displayed by the ships of the Confederacy from 1861 to 1863.

374. The navy jack of the Southern Confederacy, used after May 1, 1863, had an oblong red field, with a blue St. Andrew's cross bordered by white and having three stars on each arm and one at the intersection. It was merely the square canton of the second flag of the Confederacy elongated, so that its length was one and a half times its width. The battle flag of the Confederacy during the same period was like this navy jack, except that it was square, and all four of its sides were bordered by a white stripe one and a half inches wide. The battle flag carried by the infantry was forty-eight inches square, that by the artillery thirty-six inches, and that by the cavalry thirty inches square.

375. The national flag of the Confederacy between May 1, 1863, and March 4, 1865, had a white field twice as long as wide, with the battle flag as its union.

376. The Confederacy's national flag, adopted March 8, 1865, was the same as that adopted May 1, 1863 (375), except that one-half of the field between the union and the end of the fly was occupied by a horizontal bar of red.

377. HUDSON'S FLAG.—When Henry Hudson glided into the unsailed waters of New York harbor in his little *Half Moon*, this flag was his ensign; thus it is supposed to have been one of the first European flags reflected in the waters of what is now the busiest port on earth. It was the flag of the Netherlands, with the letters A. O. C. added to the central stripe. These were the initials of the Dutch East India Company, "Algemeene Oost-Indise Compagnie," under whose auspices Hudson sailed. Later it floated over the little huts built by the East India Company on Manhattan Island for the

GUATEMALA ENSIGN
482

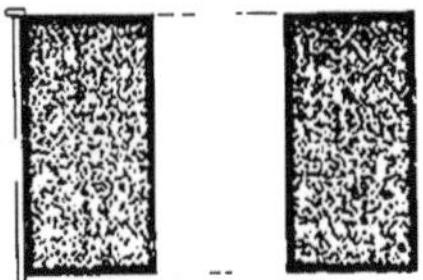
GUATEMALA MERCHANT
483

HONDURAS ENSIGN
484

HONDURAS MERCHANT
485

HAITI COAT ARMS
486

GUATEMALA COAT ARMS
487

HONDURAS COAT ARMS
488

MEXICO COAT ARMS
489

HAITI ENSIGN
490

HAITI MERCHANT
491

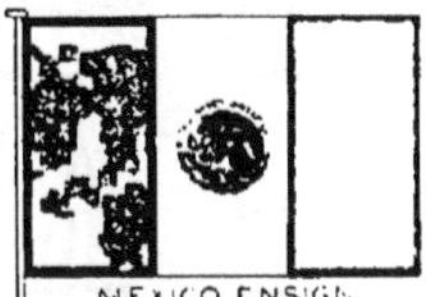
MEXICO ENSIGN
492

MEXICO MERCHANT
493

NICARAGUA ENSIGN
494

NICARAGUA MERCHANT
495

PANAMA COAT ARMS
496

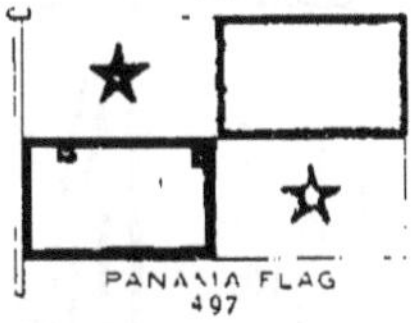
PANAMA FLAG
497

NICARAGUA COAT ARMS
498

PERU COAT ARMS
499

PARAGUAY COAT ARMS
500

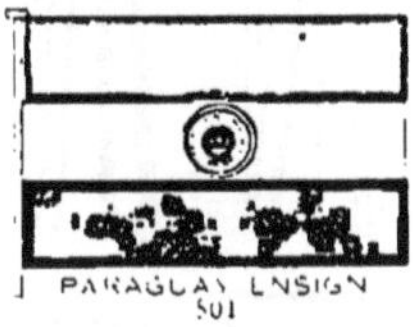
PARAGUAY ENSIGN
501

PERU
ENSIGN & PRESIDENT
502

PERU MERCHANT
503

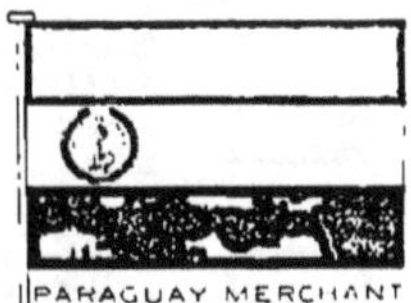
PARAGUAY MERCHANT
504

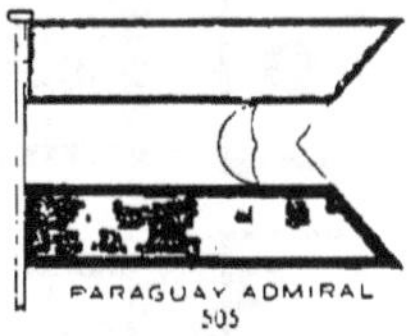
PARAGUAY ADMIRAL
505

SALVADOR ENSIGN
506

SALVADOR MERCHANT
507

URUGUAY
508

URUGUAY COAT ARMS
509

SALVADOR COAT ARMS
510

VENEZUELA COAT ARMS
511

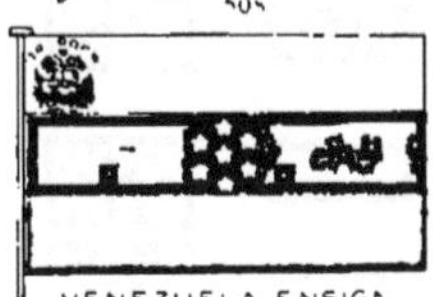
VENEZUELA ENSIGN
512

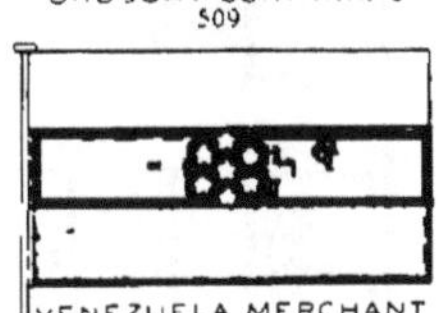
VENEZUELA MERCHANT
513

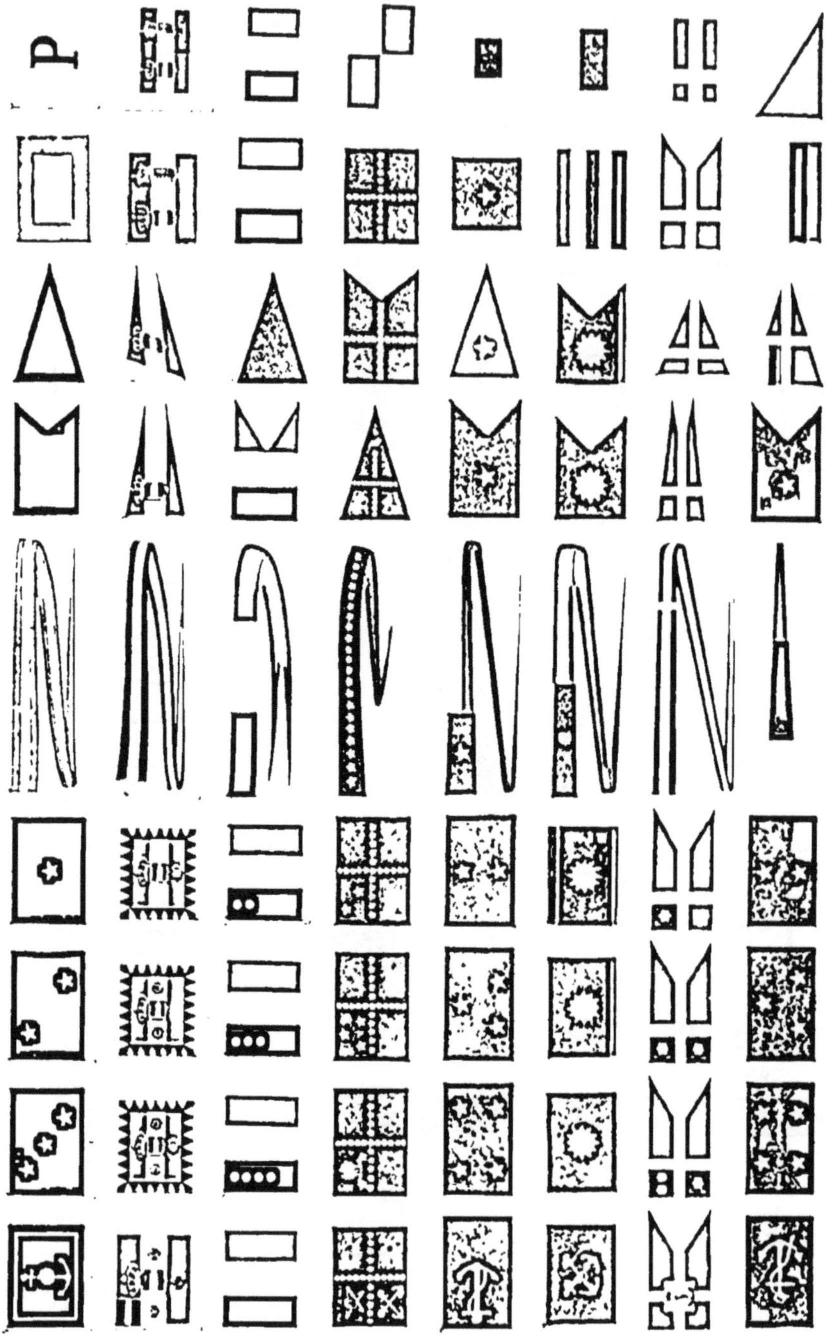
P

government organized all of New England as a royal domain. In 1686 Edmund Andros arrived as Governor of the province. The flag under his rule was the red cross of St George on a white field with a gold crown in the center. Under the crown appeared the letters J R, the cipher of King James. But in 1689, with the arrival in England of William of Orange, the colonists deposed Andros and this flag was consigned to the oblivion of banners no longer expressive of the feelings of a developing people.

386. Nova Scotia.—Nova Scotia was the New Scotland just as the Massachusetts group of colonies was the New England; for even in the days of King James there was no Great Britain, but the two separate countries. And that is why the vertical cross of St George appeared on the Andros and other New England flags, while the diagonal Scottish cross of St Andrew marked those of Nova Scotia. The center of the flag is marked by the crown and cipher of James Sixth of Scotland and First of England. He it was who united the two crosses into the union flag of 1606, the very year in which he gave the first royal grants of land in North America under which permanent settlements grew up. It was not until 1801, long after the Stars and Stripes were known on every sea, that the red diagonal cross of St Patrick, in recognition of Ireland, was added to the combined crosses, thus making the familiar British union jack of today.

387. Ensign of New England.—Early in the life of the New England Colonies it was seen that the merchant ships of the mother country needed a special flag to distinguish them from the King's ships. In 1701 we find this order from the Admiralty Office at Whitehall, London: "Merchant ships to wear no other jack than that worn by His Majesty's ships, with the distinction of a white escutcheon in the middle thereof." The Governors of His Majesty's plantations were ordered to oblige the commanders of the merchant ships to use this red ensign. The merchant ships, however, continued to fly the variants they considered to their commanders' associations. Many of them seem to have preferred the usual red or blue New England flag, which had a red St George's cross and a globe (388) or tree (pine) on a white ground in the upper hoist canton.

388. (See 387.)

389. Colonel Moultrie's Flag.—In September, 1775, Colonel William Moultrie, having received orders from the Council of Safety to take Fort Johnson on James Island, S. C., and having no flag, he designed a large blue flag with a white crescent in the upper corner next the staff. This design being suggested by the blue uniforms of the garrison and the silver crescents which the men wore on their caps, inscribed with the words "Liberty or Death." Colonel Moultrie in his memoirs states that this was the first American flag displayed in the South. (See also 390.)

390. (See 389.)

391. Washington's Navy, 1775.—This was the flag flown by Washington's six cruisers in 1775. The *Lady Washington*, a brig fitted out in 1775, was captured by H. M. S. *Fowey* on December 7 of the same year, and her colors were placed in the Admiralty Office in London. They are described as bearing "a pale green pine tree on a field of white bunting, with the motto, 'Appeal to Heaven.'" After the Continental ensign (364) came into use by Washington's fleet, January 1, 1776, this white flag and green pine tree, with variations (399), was adopted April 29, 1776, as the ensign of the vessels of the Massachusetts navy (see 399 and 401; see also the history of our Stars and Stripes printed elsewhere in this number).

392. Bedford Flag.—Probably the most interesting flag of all the colonial period is this standard of the Bedford Minute Men, carried by them at the battle of Concord. It is small, being only about 2½ feet square, but carries woven among its faded threads the love and veneration of a grateful America. Wrought in silver and gold on a red ground is an arm appearing from a cloud, with the hand holding a sword. The scroll is in gold, with the motto, "Vince Aut Morire" (Conquer or die). It now has an honored place among the relics of the Historical Society at Bedford, Mass. It bears a striking resemblance to the Ostend Eight ensign (1141).

393. Philadelphia Light Horse.—This standard, presented to the Philadelphia troop of Light Horse by Capt. Abraham Markoe and still displayed at the troop's anniversary dinners, is one of the first American flags in which thirteen stripes were used. This banner was carried by the Philadelphia troop when it escorted General Washington from Philadelphia to New York on his way to Cambridge, there to assume command of the Continental Army. The Philadelphia troop was composed of 28 men, who equipped themselves at their own expense. Captain Markoe resigned his commission as captain of this organization late in 1775, in obedience to an edict of King Christian VII of Denmark, who forbade any of his subjects to engage in the war against Great Britain. Before tendering his resignation, however, the commander presented this standard to the troop.

394. New York.—The armed ships of New York are reported to have used this flag in 1775. The beaver reminds us eloquently of the prominent part the lucrative fur trade played in the early history of the colony. The glowing accounts brought back by Hudson of the rich harvest of valuable furs to be secured led Holland to authorize the trading companies which colonized New York. The beaver was used on the seal of New Netherlands and found a place on the seal of New York City.

395. Bennington.—At the battle of Bennington, Vt., August 16, 1777, 2,000 Green Mountain boys under Gen. John Stark practically annihilated the forces under General Baum sent to capture stores and to overawe the country. The loss of these troops was partly responsible for the failure of Burgoyne's carefully planned campaign and was one of the events that led to the open recognition of our country by France.

396. Rhode Island.—Fashioned from white silk, with thirteen stars on a canton of blue and showing a blue anchor surmounted by the

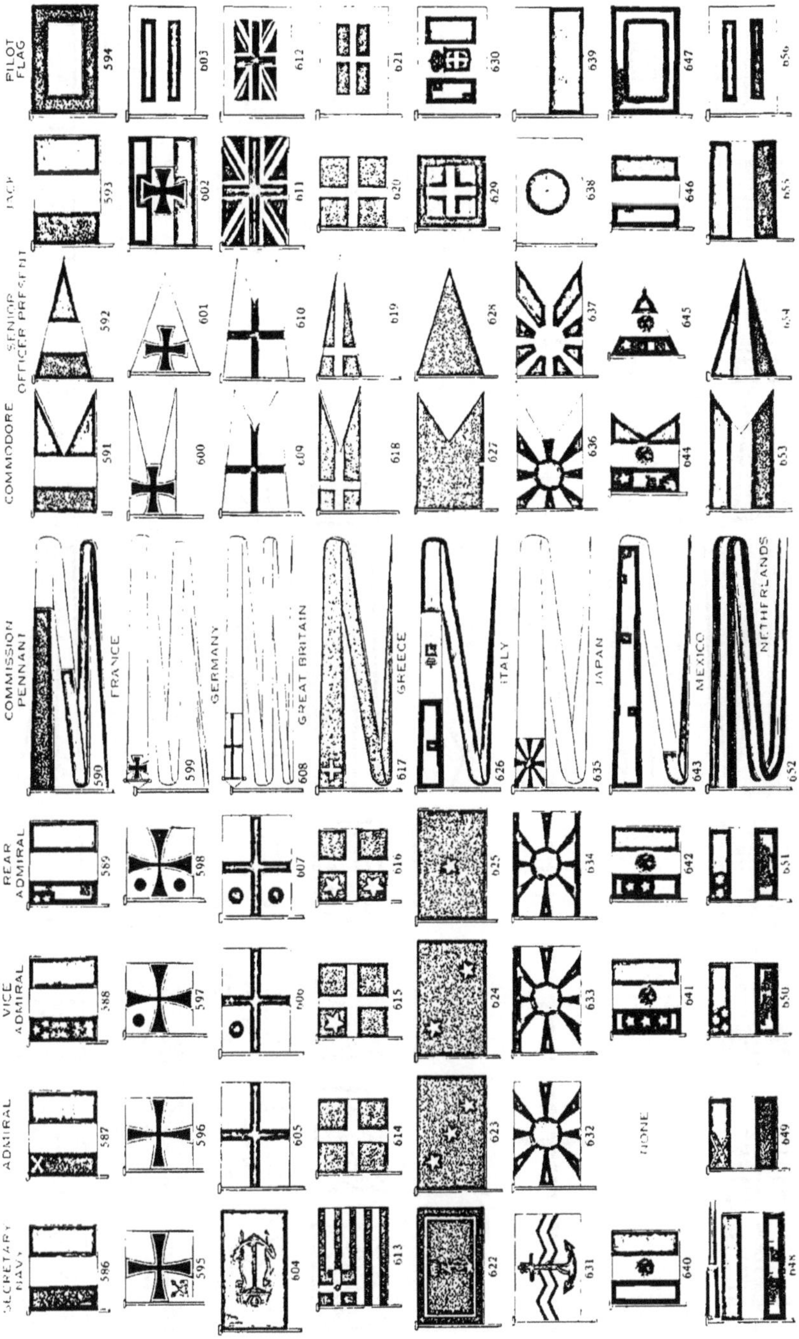
SECRETARY NAVY
ADMIRAL
VICE ADMIRAL
REAR ADMIRAL
COMMISSION PENNANT
COMMODORE
SENIOR OFFICER PRESENT
JACK
PILOT FLAG
FRANCE
GERMANY
GREAT BRITAIN
GREECE
ITALY
JAPAN
MEXICO
NETHERLANDS
NONE
586 587 588 589 590 591 592 593 594
595 596 597 598 599 600 601 602 603
604 605 606 607 608 609 610 611 612
613 614 615 616 617 618 619 620 621
622 623 624 625 626 627 628 629 630
631 632 633 634 635 636 637 638 639
640 641 642 643 644 645 646 647
648 649 650 651 652 653 654 655 656

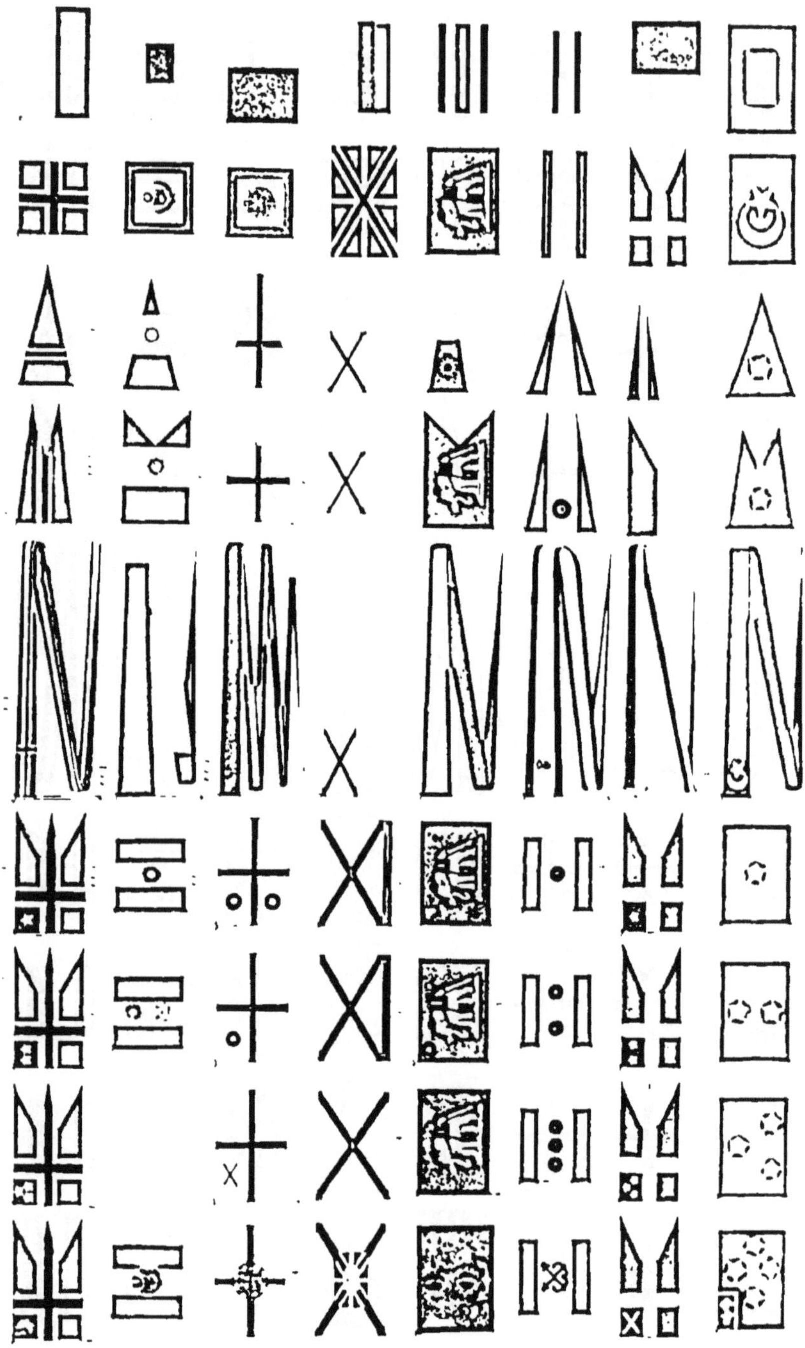

403. CONNECTICUT FLAG.—The activities of 1775 and 1776 emphasized the need of colors to distinguish the various troops. Soon after the battle of Bunker Hill the States began to make colors for themselves. Connecticut, with this flag, was one of the first. Her motto, "Qui transtulit sustinet," of which a free translation is, "God, who transported us hither, will sustain us," was put upon one side of several flags of the time, with "An Appeal to Heaven," the Massachusetts motto, upon the other. This shows almost the identical form of the permanent Connecticut flag (305).

404. MERCHANT AND PRIVATEER ENSIGN.—Those dashing privateers, whose exploits made such entertaining reading in the history books of our childhood days, flew this ensign of thirteen stripes. Many references and prints of "striped flaggs" in contemporary British literature prove its prevalence. The color of the stripes varied according to the fancy of the commanding officer. Merchant vessels nearly always displayed this flag.

405. (See 398.)

406. FORT MOULTRIE.—This flag flew from the southeast bastion of Fort Moultrie (then called Fort Sullivan), in Charleston Harbor, during the famous Revolutionary battle of June 28, 1776. Early in the attack the sky-colored emblem fell outside the parapet. Sergeant William Jasper, crying out, "Don't let us fight without a flag," vaulted over the wall under a rain of bullets, secured the flag, fixed it to a staff, and, triumphantly planting it firmly in place, leaped down within the parapet to safety. Three ringing cheers greeted his return. After an intense artillery attack lasting ten hours, the British forces were compelled to withdraw, and the next day the entire fleet left Charleston Harbor. The name of the fort was changed to Moultrie in honor of the gallant defender. This victory left the Southern States secure from invasion for more than two years. This flag is identical with Colonel Moultrie's earlier flag (380) first raised in September, 1775, with the addition of the word "Liberty" in white letters.

407. PULASKI.—Brave and gallant Count Pulaski, who gave his life for our cause in 1779, fought beneath this banner. A Polish count volunteering as a private, distinguished by his coolness and courage at the battle of Brandywine,—he was made Chief of Dragoons, with the rank of Brigadier-General. The Moravian Sisters, of Bethlehem, Pennsylvania, embroidered this flag for him. One side bears the words "Unitas Virtus Forcior" (which last word, by the way, should be *fortior*), "Union makes valor stronger," encircling the letters U. S. The other side bears the motto, "Non Alius Regit," "No other governs," with the all-seeing eye in the center triangle. Pulaski raised his own independent corps of infantry and light cavalry, and later commanded the French and American forces at the siege of Savannah, where he was mortally wounded. Thus fell, at the early age of 31, one of the many heroic foreign brothers who fought with us for liberty.

408, 409. NEW HAMPSHIRE REGIMENT.—These two New Hampshire flags belonged to the Second Regiment of the State. They were taken at Fort Anne by the British Ninth Regiment of Foot, commanded by Lieutenant Colonel Hill, a few weeks before the decisive battle of Saratoga. After the surrender of Burgoyne, Colonel Hill carried them to England, where they were treasured by his descendants, finally falling into the hands of Col. George W. Rogers, of Wykeham, Sussex. From him they were purchased in 1912 by Mr. Edward Tuck, and presented to the New Hampshire Historical Society. They are of the same size, approximately five by five and one-half feet.

The buff flag (408) with a golden disk in the center bears the motto, "We are one." From the disk radiate thirteen rays and thirteen thin lines, each line touching a golden ring in the outer circle, with each ring bearing the name of one of the thirteen States. In the upper left corner are eight red and pale blue triangles which form two crosses.

The blue silk flag with the gold fringe (409) bears the letters N. H., with "2nd Regt." below them on the small red shield in the center. The motto on the scroll is significant, "The glory, not the prey." The two crosses combined in the upper corner are of red and gold.

These two New Hampshire flags are probably the only ones now in existence which were captured during the Revolutionary War.

410. FIRST PENNSYLVANIA RIFLES.—"A deep green ground, the device a tiger, partly enclosed by toils, attempting the pass, defended by a hunter with a spear (in white) on a crimson field"—thus reads the description of the standard of the First Pennsylvania Rifles, in the words of Lieutenant Colonel Hand, written March 8, 1776. During the war this regiment served in every one of the thirteen colonies, and this banner waved at many a famous battle—at Trenton, Princeton, Brandywine, Monmouth, and Yorktown, to mention only a few.

411. THIRD MARYLAND.—The existence of this national flag, known to have been used as a regimental flag in the Revolution, sheds a bit of light on the darkness surrounding the extent to which the stars and stripes were used at the time. It is certain that this identical flag was carried by the Third Maryland Regiment at the battle of Cowpens, in January, 1778. William Bachelor was the color-bearer. It is made of thin cotton, and is remarkably well preserved. It is a little over five feet long, and almost a yard wide, and is now in the flag room of the capitol at Annapolis. It is the only instance of the use of the "Stars and Stripes" as a color (*i. e.*, by land troops), national or regimental, during the Revolutionary War, that of 1812, and the Mexican War. (See history of Stars and Stripes printed elsewhere in this number.)

412. EUTAW STANDARD.—This square of brilliant crimson formed the battle flag of Col. William Washington's cavalry troop, and led the way to victory at Cowpens and at the final battle of the Revolution, Eutaw Springs, in 1781—two decisive battles of the war in the South. Tradition tells a quaint story of its origin. It seems that Colonel Washington, on a hurried visit to his *fiancée*, Miss Jane Elliot, of South Carolina, mentioned that he had no flag. With quick flashes of her scissors, she

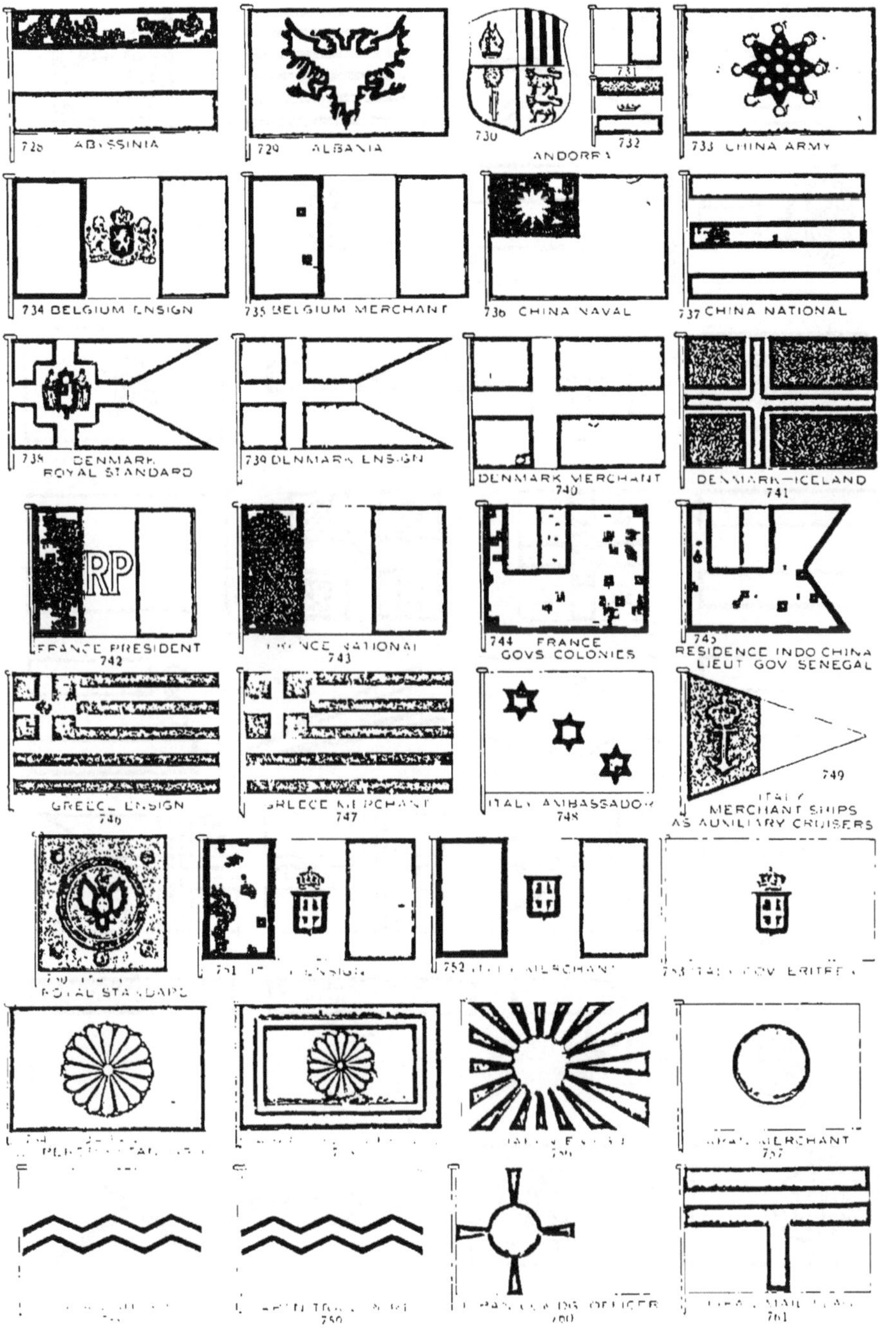
728 ABYSSINIA
729 ALBANIA
730 ANDORRA 731 732
733 CHINA ARMY
734 BELGIUM ENSIGN
735 BELGIUM MERCHANT
736 CHINA NAVAL
737 CHINA NATIONAL
738 DENMARK ROYAL STANDARD
739 DENMARK ENSIGN
DENMARK MERCHANT 740
DENMARK—ICELAND 741
FRANCE PRESIDENT 742
743
744 FRANCE GOVS COLONIES
745 RESIDENCE INDO CHINA LIEUT GOV SENEGAL
GREECE ENSIGN
747
748
749 MERCHANT SHIPS AS AUXILIARY CRUISERS
ROYAL STANDARD
751
752
753
MERCHANT 757
760
761

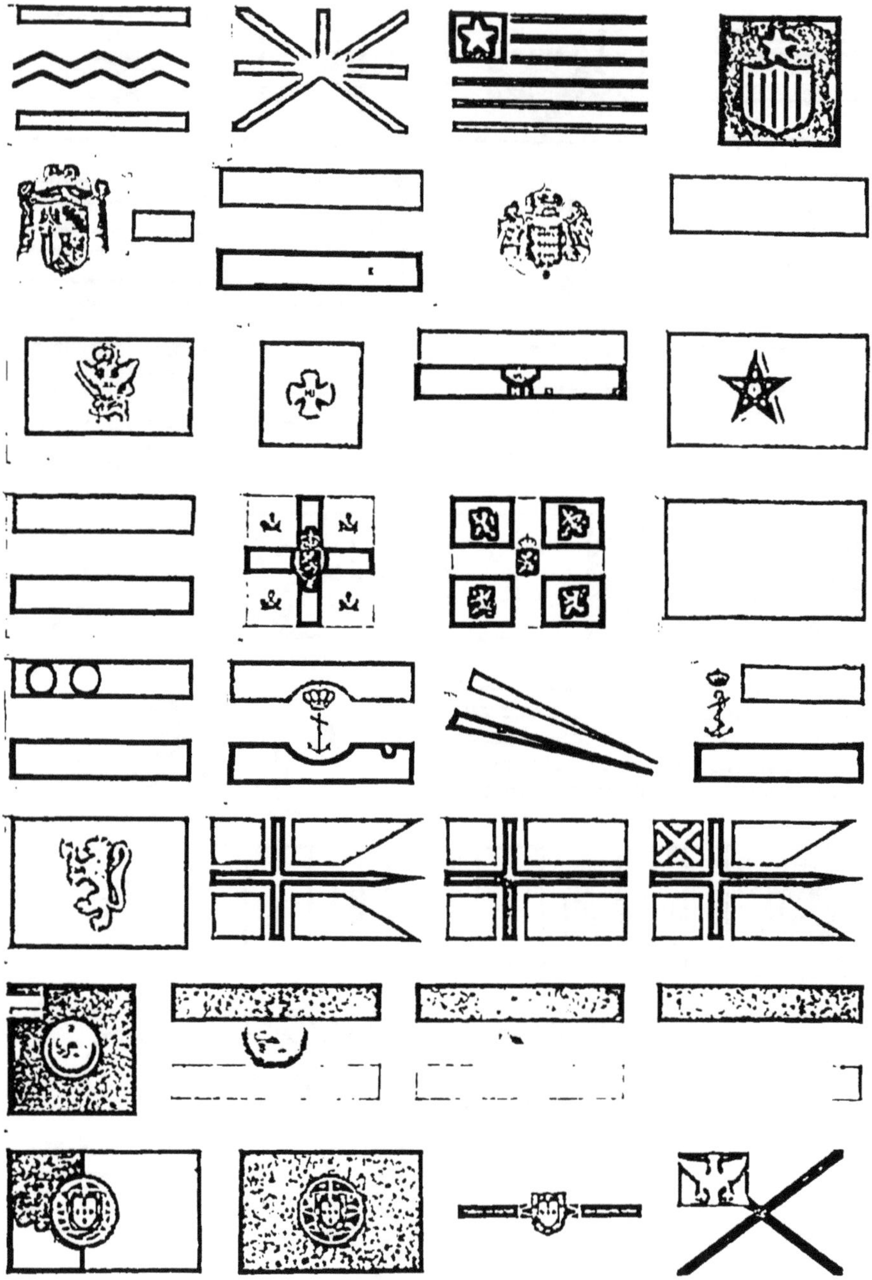

Indies in the summer of 1781 entered the Chesapeake and met the fleet of Admiral Thomas Graves, compelling him to return to New York for refitting and repairs. Then by blocking the mouths of the York and James rivers, he succeeded in cutting off communication between the British forces at Yorktown and those at New York and thus assisted materially in causing the famous surrender that closed the war (see NATIONAL GEOGRAPHIC MAGAZINE, June, 1917, pages 527-581).

423. NAPOLEON'S FLAG, LOUISIANA, 1803.—Among the many changes of flag that helped to make romantic the early history of Louisiana, this of Napoleon stands out as memorable because it was hauled down to give place for "Old Glory" on the 20th of December, 1803.

Each of the colors of this flag is woven into the history of French career by several threads. The blue banner of St. Martin was first used by the kings of France in the fourth century, and for 600 years was carried into battle as a sure omen of victory. Next came the well-loved Oriflamme, the gold-bordered banner of St. Denis. This in turn gave place to the "cornette blanche," a plain white flag emblematic of the Virgin Mary, carried by Joan of Arc and later adopted by the Bourbons.

So it was not purely an accident that the choice of the populace, storming the Bastille, in 1789, should have been the tricolor, and it is easy to see how the historic associations as well as the beauty and simplicity of the banner itself made it the permanent emblem of France.

It was fourteen years after this tricolor had become the national flag of France that the remarkable and startling [illegible] of events occurring [illegible] of the [illegible] the world from our [illegible] of Waters made it possible for us to purchase the wonderful Louisiana country.

424. RUSSIAN-AMERICAN COMPANY, ALASKA.—Although the Alaskan coast was explored in 1741, it was not until 1794 that the first and even then only partially accurate chart of the Alaskan mainland was made. Kodiak was settled in 1784, and in the succeeding years private traders raided and robbed the Indian villages until the reign of lawlessness was checked by the formation in 1799 of the Russian-American Company, which remained dominant in Alaskan affairs for sixty years. And thus it was that while the young American Republic was getting on its feet and meeting its first problems of administration and expansion this white, blue, and red standard was [illegible] over a ship-[illegible] the long days of Alaskan summers and [illegible] of many trading posts under the [illegible] of the long winter nights. In 1867 the Alaska purchase placed our own starry flag on these valuable [illegible] northern shores.

425. AZTEC STANDARD.—BATTLE OF OTUMBA.—History says that Cortes and his Spaniards with [illegible] allies the Tlascalans, were on the verge of defeat at the battle of Otumba when the Spanish leader, observing the gorgeously decorated litter of the Aztec general, and discovering that he carried the battle standard lashed to his back, summoned several cavaliers, and praying to Santiago (429) they fought their way to the Aztec's side. Cortes overthrew the general and Salamanca cut the standard from his back. The loss of their emblem demoralized the Aztec forces and turned the tide of the battle. Cortes afterward presented the standard to the Tlascalan chieftain Maxixca as a reward for his aid and friendship, and the Spanish King caused it to be represented on Salamanca's coat-of-arms. This illustration of the standard, which was called the Quetzaltecpamitl and was composed of a golden sun surrounded by the richest plumes of the quetzal (see 857), was taken from the picture writings of the Tlascallans, shown in the Lienzo of Tlascalla (see 426).

426. BANNERS, MEXICAN.—The Lienzo of Tlascala is a document of great importance, as it represents in hieroglyphics the principal events of the conquest of Mexico painted by the Indians themselves. It is on long bands of linen and is divided into 80 illustrations by perpendicular lines. The Tlascallans were a fierce mountain people, implacable foes of the Aztecs, and became the staunch allies of Cortes after their armies were decisively defeated by the Spaniards on their way to Tenochtitlan. In numerous of these illustrations Cortes and his cavaliers are shown in battle, dressed in their armor and astride their prancing steeds, while by their sides are shown their Tlascallan allies, armed with their crude native weapons and carrying their beautiful banners (426), cleverly constructed of precious metals and bright-colored plumes, mounted on wooden staffs and lashed to their backs to allow free use of both arms.

427. BANNERS—INCAS, BEFORE PIZARRO.—The Children of the Sun, as the Incas were called, lived among the mountain fastnesses of Peru and were as cultured as the Aztecs of Mexico. Their country has been called the "Ophir of the Occident," and well it deserved the name, for its treasures of precious metals exceeded the dreams of avarice. Like the Aztecs, these ancient Peruvians used the gaudy plumage of tropical birds for decorative purposes, and this sketch of two old banners illustrates the feathered bedands and trimming. These Sun worshipers also had great reverence for the rainbow and used a representation of it in their royal insignia. An old description referring to the ceremony incident to the recognition of the heir apparent says: "Being crowned, as of age, he was given command of his father's armies and was entitled to display the royal standard of the rainbow in his military expeditions."

428. CORTES' STANDARD.—The hardy and romantic adventurers who followed in the wake of Columbus were not merely sordid gold hunters; they were the descendants of soldiers who had for centuries fought in the holy wars of the Cross against the Crescent, and in their veins flowed the blood of the knight-errant and Crusader. Gold they sought with eagerness and without scruple, but they wanted glory almost as much as they wanted gold, and in the pursuit of both they carried aloft the banner of the Church.

Around the edge of this standard of Cortes there appears in Spanish: "This standard was

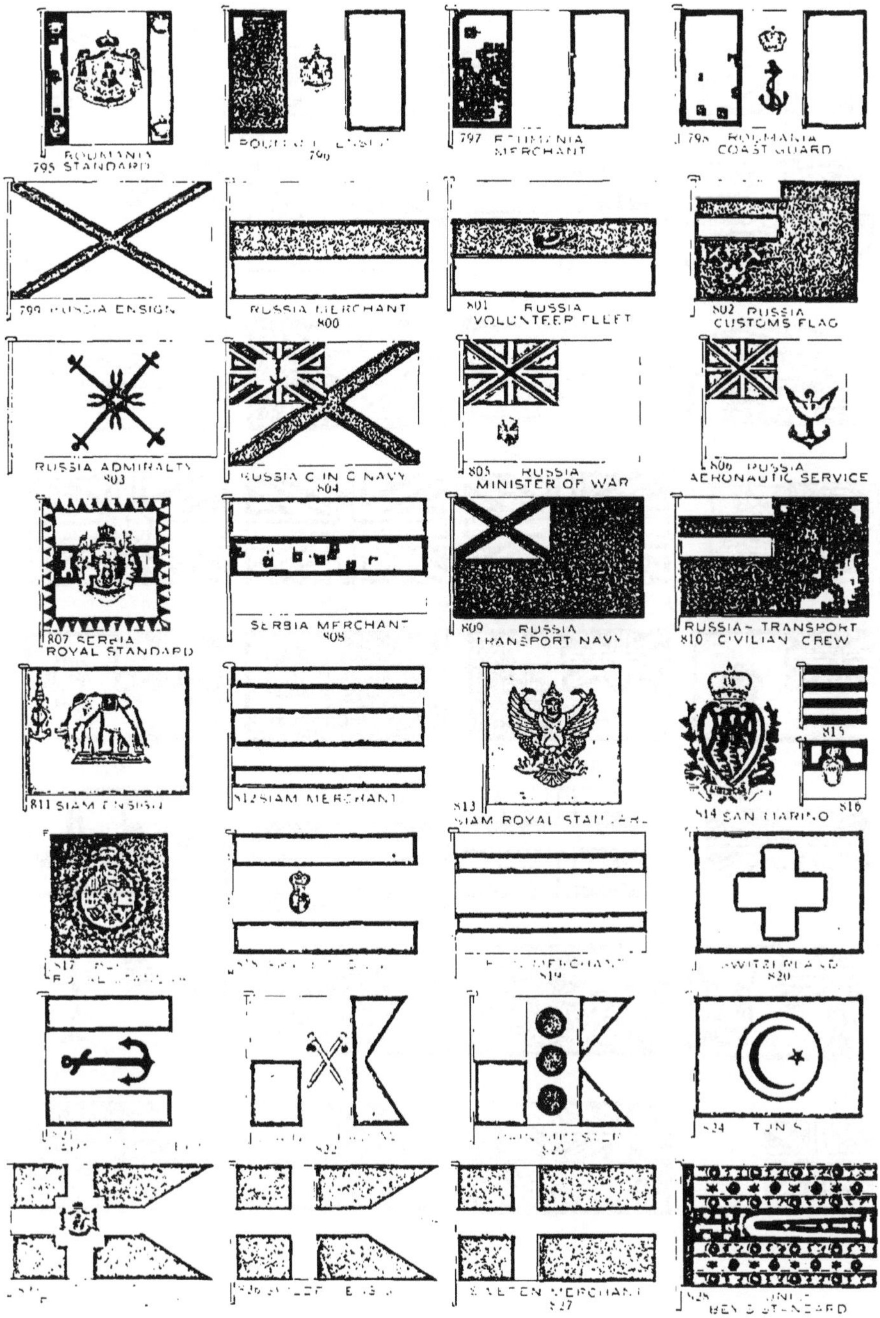
795 ROUMANIA STANDARD
796
797 ROUMANIA MERCHANT
798 ROUMANIA COAST GUARD
799 RUSSIA ENSIGN
RUSSIA MERCHANT 800
801 RUSSIA VOLUNTEER FLEET
802 RUSSIA CUSTOMS FLAG
RUSSIA ADMIRALTY 803
RUSSIA C IN C NAVY 804
805 RUSSIA MINISTER OF WAR
806 RUSSIA AERONAUTIC SERVICE
807 SERBIA ROYAL STANDARD
SERBIA MERCHANT 808
809 RUSSIA TRANSPORT NAVY
RUSSIA – TRANSPORT 810 CIVILIAN CREW
811 SIAM ENSIGN
812 SIAM MERCHANT
813 SIAM ROYAL STANDARD
815
814 SAN MARINO
816
817
MERCHANT 819
SWITZERLAND 820
824 TUNIS
826 ENSIGN
MERCHANT 827
828 STANDARD

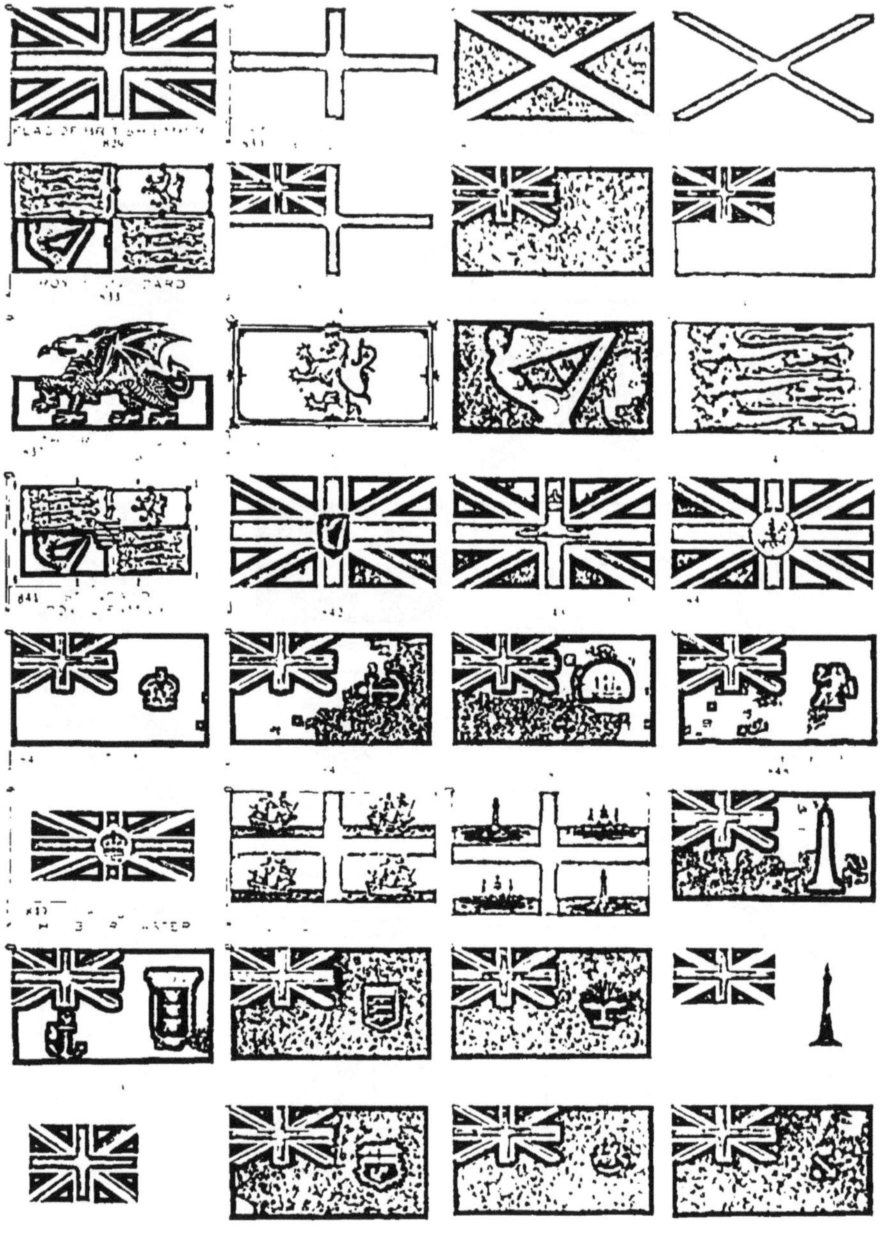

patron saint of Mexico, and was flown in triumph for a time; but disaster overtook him and, with several of his generals, he was shot to death at Chihuahua in 1811. Two subsequent revolutions were also led by priests, *Padres* Morelos and Mier, and they, too, met Hidalgo's fate. They died upon the threshold of success, however, for Mexican independence of Spain was accomplished in 1821. The banner of Hidalgo is preserved in the National Museum in Mexico City.

435. TREATY OF TORDESILLAS.—These flags appearing on maps of the sixteenth century indicate the division of territory for exploration and conquest by Spain and Portugal effected by the Treaty of Tordesillas in 1494. Pope Nicholas V had given the Portuguese exclusive right to the "road to the Indies" in 1454, but he had in mind only the coast of Africa. Complicating the situation came the discovery of land in the west by Columbus, who believed that he had found the eastern shores of Asia. Pope Alexander VI, a Spaniard, was appealed to and he drew a line north to south a hundred leagues west of the Azores, giving the Spaniards the right to all that lay beyond. The Portuguese protested and the diplomats met at Tordesillas, Spain, with the result that the line was shifted 270 leagues farther west, approximating the 50th meridian of longitude west of Greenwich. This line strikes South America at the mouth of the Amazon, and the Spaniards therefore laid claim to the greater part of the continent and sought to exclude all other nations. This probably explains why Portugal secured only Brazil from all this vast domain.

436. ORDER OF CHRIST.—This flag is to be found on old maps of Brazil, where it indicates the control of territory by the members of the Brazilian section of this ancient order, which was instituted by Denys, King of Portugal, in 1231, to expel the Moors from Betica, adjoining Portugal. According to eighteenth century historians, the order "added many gallant Countries in Asia, Africk, and Brazil, to the domains of Portugal, and so improved their own Estates, that all the Isles in the Atlantick do belong to them; besides the Rents of the Mine of St. George in Guinea, amounting to 100,000 Ducats of yearly Income."

437. BRAZIL EMPIRE.—Driven from their kingdom by the invading armies of Napoleon, the royal family of Portugal in 1808 took refuge in Brazil, and for the first time in the history of the world a colony became the seat of government of its mother country. The prince regent, coming to the throne as Dom John VI, raised this standard of empire. In 1889 the colonists threw off the imperial yoke and established a republic, retaining in their national ensign (see 458) some of the characteristic features of the empire flag—the yellow diamond and the green field. The shield and imperial crown of the old flag, however, were replaced by the blue globe and the republican motto, "Ordem e Progresso."

438. SPANISH FLAG IN MEXICO.—The old flag from which this illustration has been made was carried by Spanish troops in the war of Mexican independence and it now reposes, among other relics of that struggle, in the museum at Mexico City. Its peculiar design is an adaptation of the raguled cross of the Spanish Bourbons, which may also be seen in the earlier flags of Ostend and Biscay (1143 and 1146), but with an added feature of crown-crested coats-of-arms on the ends of the cross.

439. MEXICO FLAG.—Migrating Aztecs, successors to the Toltecs in Mexico, in 1325 came to the shores of a lake in the valley of Mexico, or Anahuac, and there, as had been foretold by their oracle, "they beheld, perched on the stem of a prickly pear, which shot out from the crevices of a rock that was washed by the waves, a royal eagle of extraordinary size and beauty, with a serpent in his talons and his broad wings open to the sun." This determined the location of Tenochtitlan, now the City of Mexico. From this legend was devised the coat-of-arms which appears in the center of this flag, adopted when Mexico became independent, in 1821 (see new coat-of-arms and Mexican flags 489-492-493).

440. ALAMO FLAG.—This was the flag that floated in 1836 over the historic mission fortress, the Alamo, at San Antonio, when Texas was fighting for her independence. For twelve days the garrison of 178 Americans held out under the heavy bombardment of a force of 4,000 Mexicans. On the 6th of March the garrison was so weakened that the Mexicans were able to make assaults. Twice beaten back, the invaders were successful at last only through sheer weight of numbers. They gained an entrance to find but five of the brave defenders alive. These Santa Anna ordered bayoneted in cold blood. The war cry, "Remember the Alamo," echoed over many a battlefield, leading the Texans to ultimate victory. The date indicated the adherence to the constitution of 1824, and for this reason the numbers were used in place of the eagle, serpent, and cactus of the Mexican national flag.

441. TEXAS FLAG (NAVAL).—When Texas seceded from Mexico and became an independent republic, the first flag that seems to have been adopted was the naval flag, with its single star and thirteen stripes, the latter evidently borrowed from her neighbor to the north, the United States. The date given for this is April 9, 1836, antedating by several months the adoption of the first national standard of Texas, the design of which was "an azure ground with a large golden star central."

As to the origin of the lone star there are several legends. One gives the honor to Henry Smith, head of the Provisional Government, who is said to have sealed his State papers with the impression of a brass button on his coat, which had in relief a single star surrounded by an oak wreath. Another story gives the credit to a Mrs. Venson, who presented a flag with that device to a Texas regiment in 1836 (see State flag 328).

442-443. NEW GRANADA (COLOMBIA).—These were the flags of New Granada, the confederation of South American States now mainly embraced in the Republic of Colombia. In 1863 these States effected a closer union and changed their flag from three broad vertical stripes of yellow, blue, and red to the present Colombian flags (shown in 462-463). The old and new ensigns (442 and 462) are much

THE FLAGS OF PAN-AMERICA

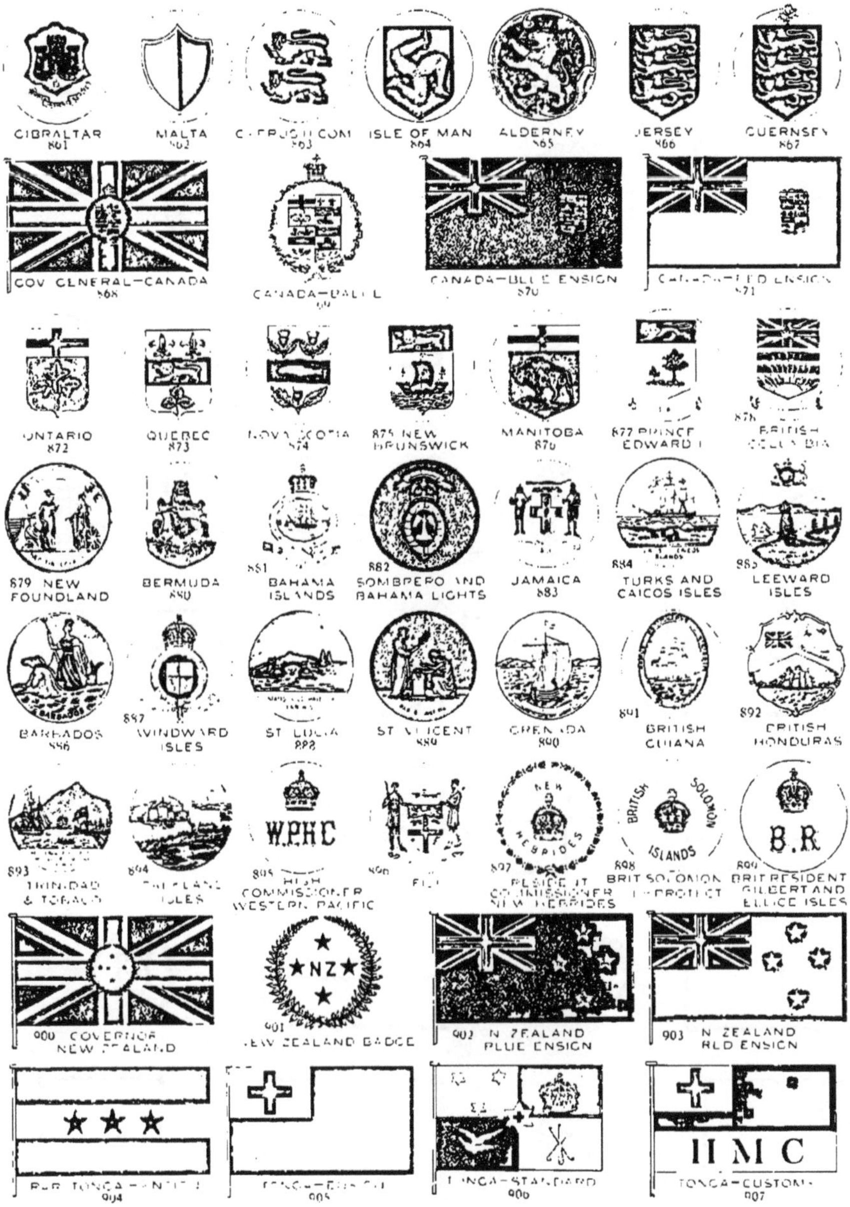
GIBRALTAR 861
MALTA 862
CYPRUS HI COM 863
ISLE OF MAN 864
ALDERNEY 865
JERSEY 866
GUERNSEY 867
GOV GENERAL—CANADA 868
CANADA—BADGE 869
CANADA—BLUE ENSIGN 870
CANADA—RED ENSIGN 871
ONTARIO 872
QUEBEC 873
NOVA SCOTIA 874
875 NEW BRUNSWICK
MANITOBA 876
877 PRINCE EDWARD I
878 BRITISH COLUMBIA
879 NEW FOUNDLAND
BERMUDA 880
881 BAHAMA ISLANDS
882 SOMBRERO AND BAHAMA LIGHTS
JAMAICA 883
884 TURKS AND CAICOS ISLES
885 LEEWARD ISLES
BARBADOS 886
887 WINDWARD ISLES
ST LUCIA 888
ST VINCENT 889
GRENADA 890
891 BRITISH GUIANA
892 BRITISH HONDURAS
893 TRINIDAD & TOBAGO
894 FALKLAND ISLES
W.P.H.C
895 HIGH COMMISSIONER WESTERN PACIFIC
896 FIJI
NEW HEBRIDES
897 RESIDENT COMMISSIONER NEW HEBRIDES
BRITISH SOLOMON ISLANDS
898 BRIT SOLOMON I PROTECT
B.R
899 BRIT RESIDENT GILBERT AND ELLICE ISLES
900 GOVERNOR NEW ZEALAND
NZ
901 NEW ZEALAND BADGE
902 N ZEALAND BLUE ENSIGN
903 N ZEALAND RED ENSIGN
TONGA 904
TONGA—ENSIGN 905
TONGA—STANDARD 906
HMC
TONGA—CUSTOMS 907

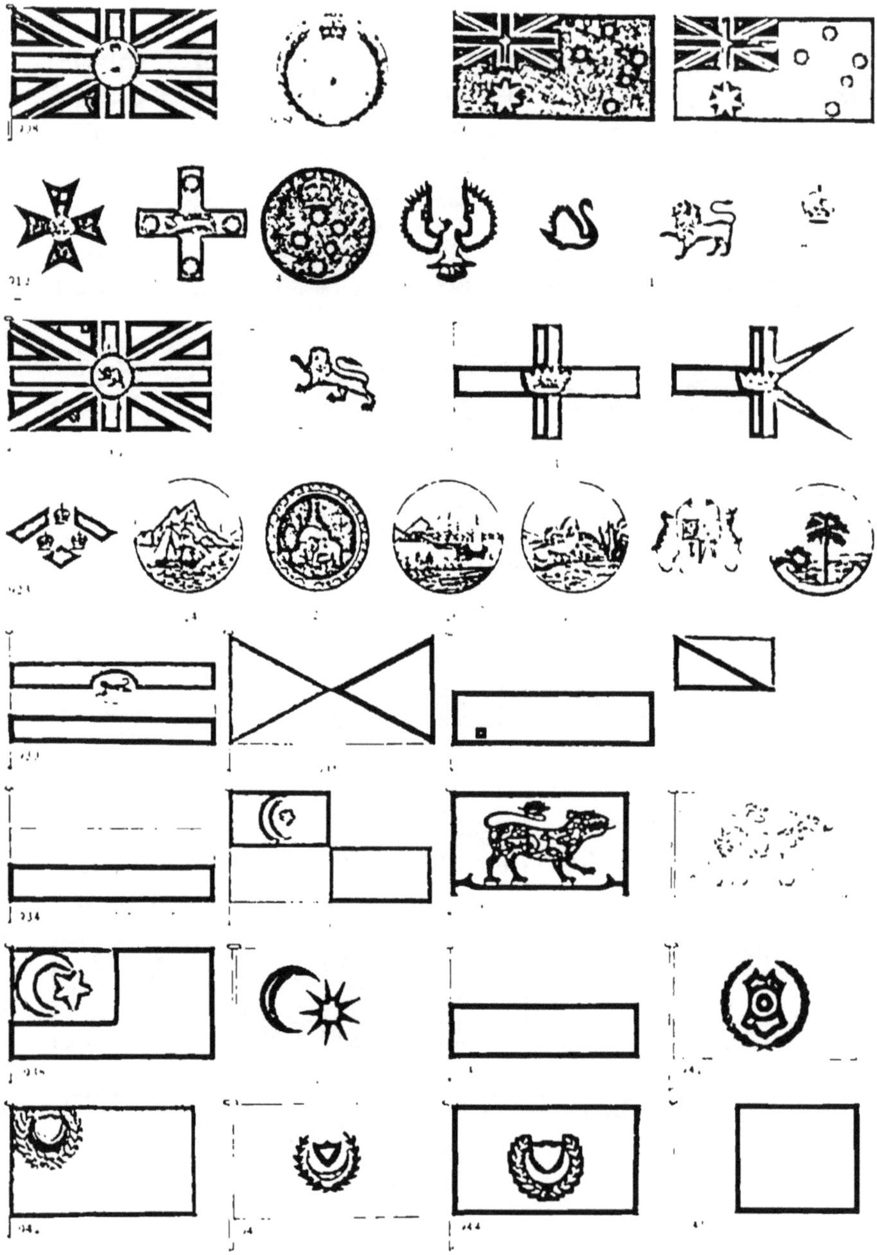

458 The present flag of Brazil was largely inherited from the extinct empire. It consists of a green field twice as long as wide on which a diamond-shaped figure is emblazoned in yellow. The green represents the vegetable kingdom and the yellow the mineral. The blue circle within the yellow diamond studded with stars is a representation of the heavens at Rio when the constellation of the Southern Cross is at the meridian. The words stamped in the course of the terrestrial orbit mean "Order and Progress."

459 The President's flag of Brazil consists of a blue field with the national coat-of-arms in the center. The large five-pointed star typifying the unity and territorial integrity of the nation is bisected in such a manner that one of the halves of each point is green and the other yellow, symbolizing respectively the vegetable and mineral wealth of the country. The blue circular band inscribed within the star contains twenty-one small silver stars, reminders of the twenty States of the Brazil in Union and the neutral city of Rio de Janeiro. The five large stars in the center of the coat-of-arms represent the constellation of the Southern Cross. The entire shield is upheld by a vertical sword, in the center of whose hilt on a red field is set a star. The shield is encircled by two branches of coffee and tobacco plants as emblems of the country's agricultural wealth, while the straight golden rays radiating in all directions outward and upward beyond the shield denote the rising of the sun that is the glorious future and destiny of Brazil. Inscribed below are the words "Estados Unidos do Brazil" (the United States of Brazil) and the date of the establishment of the republic, November 15, 1889.

460 October 18, 1917, will be the centennial of the Chilean flag. On October 18, 1817, Gen. Bernardo O'Higgins, the supreme director of Chile, decreed its adoption. It consists of a field the lower half of which is red and the upper white, with a blue canton in the upper left-hand corner occupied by a large five-pointed silver star.

461 The banner of the President of Chile consists of the national ensign with the coat-of-arms of the country thereon. The condor and [illegible] supporting the shield represent the strongest and most [illegible] land of the Chilean Andes and the most peaceful. Crown [illegible]. The [illegible] of [illegible] which crowns the shield was formerly used as a special [illegible] of the President of the Republic as a representation of the supreme executive dignity of the nation. In the old days of sailing ships the sailor who first succeeded in boarding an enemy ship of the enemy and came out of the action alive was rewarded by being crowned with a naval diadem of gold. Copies of this crown appear on the head of the condor and the [illegible]. The inscription on the coat-of-arms means "By Right or Might."

462 Colombia inherited its flag and coat-of-arms from the Republic of New Granada, of which it is the successor. Following the death of Simon Bolivar the Colombian Union set up by him, which consisted of the present republics of Venezuela, Ecuador, Colombia and Panama, ceased to exist, and New Granada, one of the succeeding States, adopted what is now the coat-of-arms and the flag of Colombia. The upper half of this flag is yellow, the lower half divided between light blue and bright red, the red strip being at the bottom. On the ensign is embroidered the national coat-of-arms.

463 The merchant flag of Colombia is a replica of the national ensign, except that instead of the coat-of-arms there appears a bright red oval surrounding a small field of blue, upon which is imposed an eight-pointed star.

464 Colombia's coat-of-arms consists of a shield divided into three horizontal sections, the upper section displaying upon a field of blue a golden pomegranate tinged with red, with the leaves and stem of the same color. On each side of the pomegranate is an inclined golden cornucopia, the one on the right pouring out toward the center gold coins and the one on the left overflowing with the fruits of the tropics. The middle section of the shield is platinum colored and bears a red liberty cap supported upon a lance. The lower section represents a silvery-waved ocean divided by the Isthmus of Panama, with full-rigged ship in both the Pacific Ocean and Caribbean Sea. The shield is supported by four national banners. The crest shows the condor of the Andes with extended wings, from its beak hanging a laurel wreath to which is attached a streamer bearing the inscription in Latin in black letters, "Liberty and Order."

465 For a description of the coat-of-arms of Chile, see 461.

466 Costa Rica's flag is made up of five stripes, blue at the top and bottom, red in the center, and white between the red and blue. The red stripe is double width. The national coat-of-arms, in diameter equal to the red stripe, is placed in the center of the field.

467 The merchant flag of Costa Rica is a duplicate of the ensign, except that the coat-of-arms is left off.

468 As revised by the decree of 1906 the coat-of-arms of Costa Rica represents three volcanoes and an extensive valley between two oceans, with a merchant ship sailing on each of them. On the extreme left of the line that marks the horizon is a rising sun. On the upper part of the field are two myrtle palms, half covered and joined by a white ribbon which contains the following inscription in gold letters: "Republica de Costa Rica." The field between the peaks of the volcanoes and the myrtle palms contains five stars of equal size arranged in an arc. The crest of the shield is a blue ribbon interlaced in the shape of a crown and bearing in silver letters the inscription, "America Central."

469 The quarantine flag of Cuba is yellow, with a black anchor and Greek cross superimposed upon the center.

470 The Cuban patriotically calls his national flag "La Estrella Solitaria," or "The Lone Star." This banner became the official emblem of Cuba on the 20th of May, 1902. It consists of a field with three blue and two white horizontal stripes, with a solitary star set in the center of a red equilateral triangle

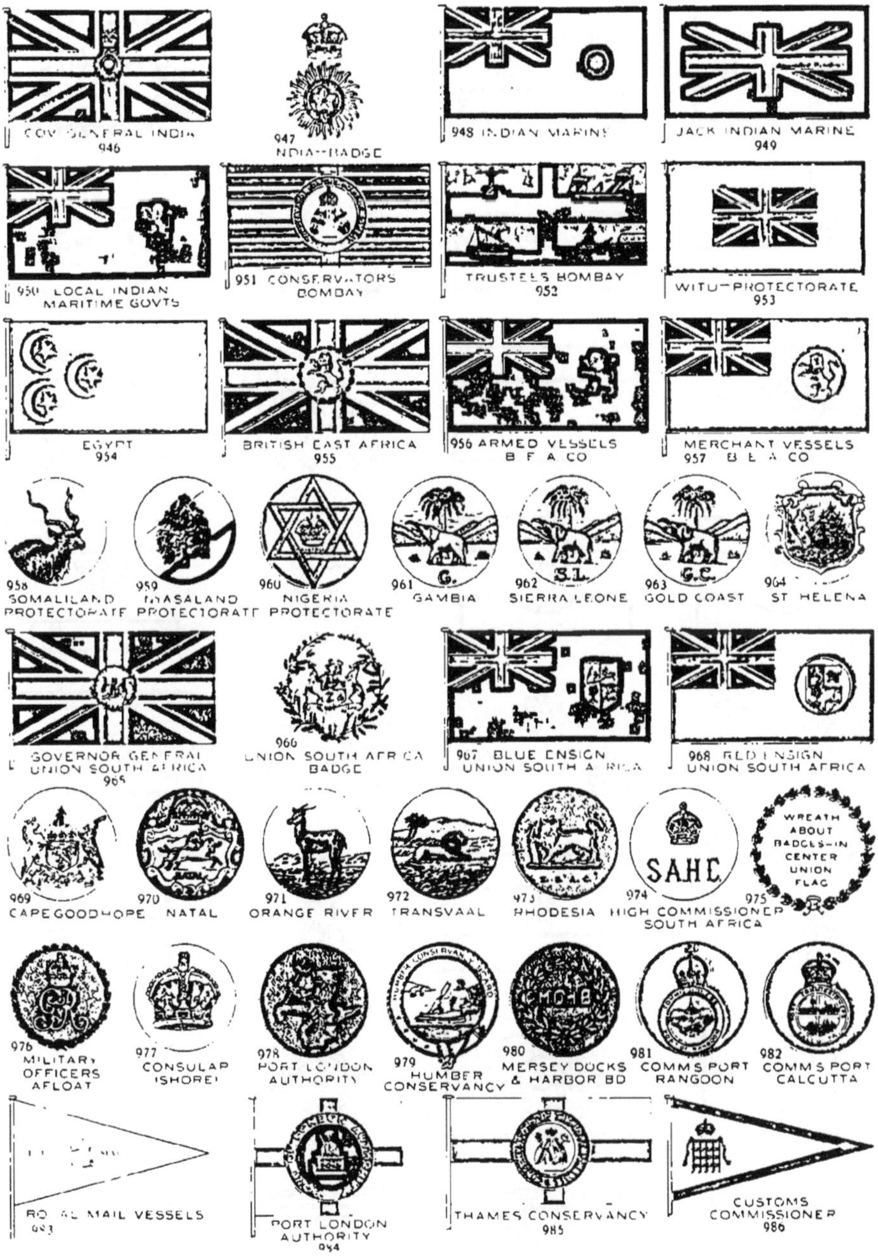
GOV GENERAL INDIA 946
947 INDIA—BADGE
948 INDIAN MARINE
JACK INDIAN MARINE 949
950 LOCAL INDIAN MARITIME GOVTS
951 CONSERVATORS BOMBAY
TRUSTEES BOMBAY 952
WITU—PROTECTORATE 953
EGYPT 954
BRITISH EAST AFRICA 955
956 ARMED VESSELS B E A CO
MERCHANT VESSELS 957 B E A CO
958 SOMALILAND PROTECTORATE
959 NYASALAND PROTECTORATE
960 NIGERIA PROTECTORATE
961 G. GAMBIA
962 S.L. SIERRA LEONE
963 G.C. GOLD COAST
964 ST HELENA
GOVERNOR GENERAL UNION SOUTH AFRICA 965
966 UNION SOUTH AFRICA BADGE
967 BLUE ENSIGN UNION SOUTH AFRICA
968 RED ENSIGN UNION SOUTH AFRICA
969 CAPE GOOD HOPE
970 NATAL
971 ORANGE RIVER
972 TRANSVAAL
973 RHODESIA
974 SAHC HIGH COMMISSIONER SOUTH AFRICA
975 WREATH ABOUT BADGES—IN CENTER UNION FLAG
976 MILITARY OFFICERS AFLOAT
977 CONSULAR (SHORE)
978 PORT LONDON AUTHORITY
979 HUMBER CONSERVANCY
980 MERSEY DOCKS & HARBOR BD
981 COMM S PORT RANGOON
982 COMM S PORT CALCUTTA
ROYAL MAIL VESSELS 983
PORT LONDON AUTHORITY 984
THAMES CONSERVANCY 985
CUSTOMS COMMISSIONER 986

taken in early life. In the ancient days of the Indians none but the royal family could wear its beautiful feathers. The tail feathers of the male, which sometimes reach a length of three feet, are of a peacock green ranging to indigo, and contrast with the scarlet breast of this proud and unconquerable bird.

488 The coat-of-arms of Honduras is an elaborate affair, with a shield supported on the mountains of the republic and surmounted by two horns of plenty, out of which all good things in tropical fruits and flowers are flowing. On the shield is a pyramid with a blazing sun rising out of the green waters of the sea. Around the shield is an inscription which reads: "Republic of Honduras—Free, Sovereign, Independent—15 Sept. 1821."

489 Mexico Coat-of-Arms.—The design for the coat-of-arms of Mexico has been changed very recently from that shown on the flag pictured in 489 to this arrangement, which shows a side view of the eagle. It is, of course, based upon the legend relating to the founding of Mexico City. It has the same fundamentals—the eagle, the serpent, the nopal cactus, and the branches of laurel and evergreen oak—but in addition has the words *Estados Unidos Mexicanos* (United States of Mexico) to round out the circle and further to identify the seal. The change was made in February, 1917, under the direction of President Carranza, the explanation given being that it conforms more closely to the ancient Aztec picture-graphs of the event.

490 The national flag of Haiti consists of a field the upper part of which is blue and the lower red, with the coat-of-arms of the country in the center. The flag was adopted in 1843.

491 The merchant flag of Haiti is blue and red, exactly like the national ensign except for the absence of the coat-of-arms.

492 Dating from 1823, the national flag of Mexico consists of three parallel vertical bars, the one next the flagstaff being green, the middle one white, and the outer one red. The three guarantees of the republic which date from that time are symbolized in the flag. The green denotes independence, the white the purity of religion, and the red the union of the Spanish element with the Mexican nation. On the white bar is placed the national coat-of-arms (see also [illegible]).

493 Mexico's merchant flag is exactly like the national ensign, except that the coat-of-arms is absent.

494 The ensign of Nicaragua consists of a field of three horizontal bars, the upper and lower blue and the middle one white, with the coat-of-arms of the country on the white bar. This flag dates from 1823 [illegible] in 1854 it was superseded by [illegible] which in its turn gave place to [illegible]. The coat-of-arms consists of a triangular shield (No. 498).

495 According to the [illegible] Pan-American Union [illegible] the merchant flag of Nicaraguan merchant vessels shall not bear the coat-of-arms on the flag.

496 The present escutcheon of the Republic of Panama is described in the Constitution. It rests upon a field of green, symbolical of vegetation. It is ogival in form and divided into three parts. The center of the shield shows the Isthmus with its two seas and the sky, wherein is depicted the moon rising over the waves, with the sun setting behind the mountains, thus marking the solemn hour of Panama's declaration of independence. The upper part is subdivided into two sections. In the right-hand section, on a silver field, appear a sword and gun so placed as to suggest abandonment, signifying an eternal farewell to the civil wars that have heretofore been the cause of the country's ruin. In the section to the left, on a field of red, appear a spade and hoe crossed to symbolize labor. The lower part of the shield is also subdivided into two sections. The right-hand section shows, on a field of azure, a cornucopia, the emblem of plenty, and in the left-hand section, on a field of silver, is a winged wheel symbolizing progress. Surmounting the shield and covering it with outstretched wings is poised an eagle, the emblem of sovereignty, its head turned to the left and holding in its beak a silver streamer, with ends flying to right and left. On the streamer is the following motto: "Pro mundi beneficio" (For the benefit of the world). Above the eagle seven golden stars are grouped in the form of an arch, representing the provinces into which the republic is divided. As decorative accessories, two national flags, gathered at the lower extremity of the staff, are stacked on either side of the shield.

497 The field of the flag of Panama is divided into four quarters. The upper quarter next to the flagstaff is white, and the lower one farthest away from the staff is also white. The lower quarter next the flagstaff is blue and the upper quarter farthest away is red. In the upper white quarter appears a blue star and in the lower white quarter a red star. Both the flag and coat-of-arms of the republic are only provisional, the constitution authorizing a contest for the adoption of a permanent design.

498 The present escutcheon of Nicaragua was borrowed from the old United Provinces of the Center of America, of which it was a member. On the base appears a range of volcanoes located upon a strip of land washed by both oceans. Surmounting these, and in the upper part of the triangle, appears a rainbow, below this a liberty cap radiating light. Around the escutcheon appears the legend in gold: "República de Nicaragua—America Central."

499 The law prescribing the coat-of-arms of Peru says: "The coat-of-arms of the Peruvian Republic shall consist of a shield divided into three fields, to wit: one of sky blue on the right, in which is a llama looking toward the left; another of white to the left, with a cinchona tree; in the base a field of red with a cornucopia from which flow coins of gold. These emblems symbolize the riches of Peru in the three natural kingdoms. The shield shall bear as a crest a civic crown (laurel wreath), and on either side a flag and a standard with the national colors."

500 Panama's coat-of-arms consists of palm and olive branches interlaced at the vertex, with a circular space between; in the center of this space is the morning star, and in

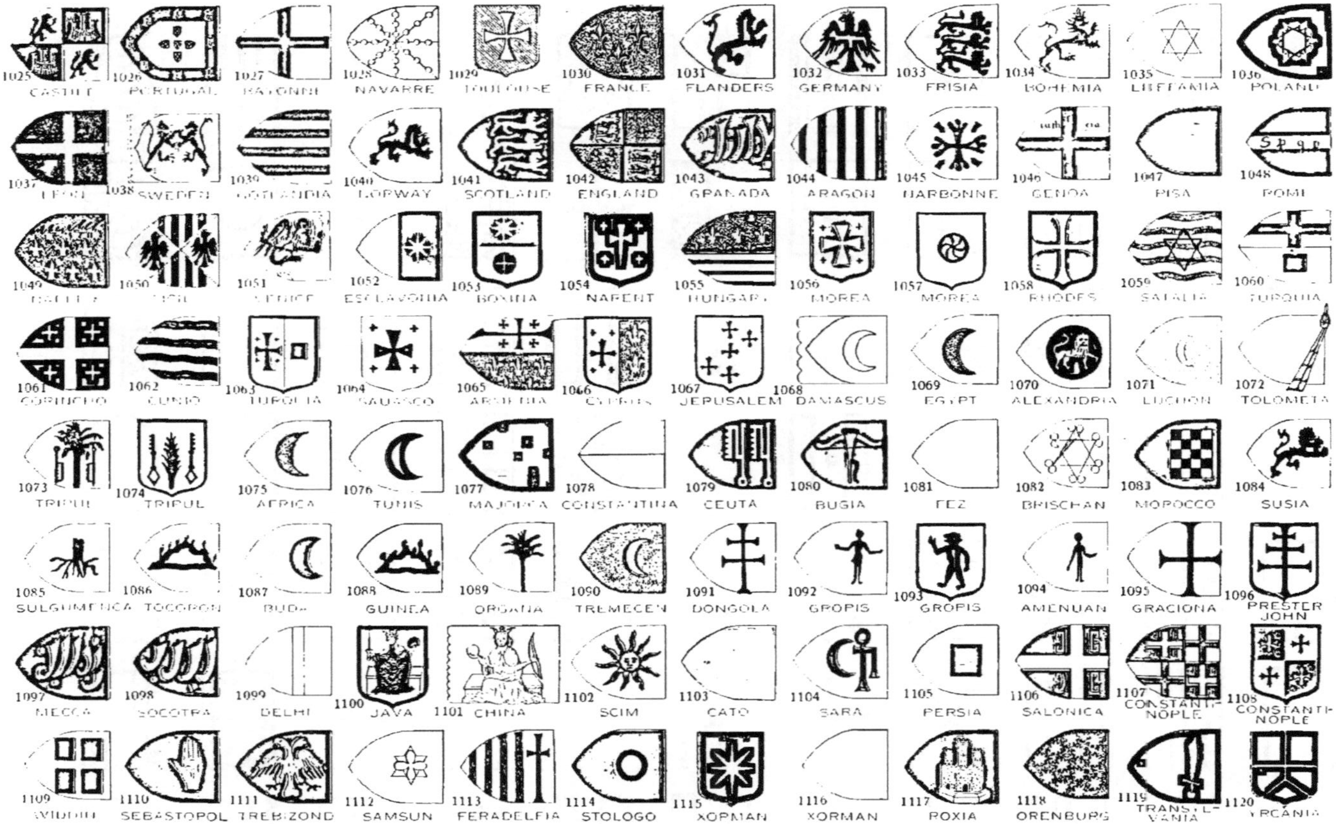

THE FLAGS OF THE WORLD FIVE HUNDRED AND SEVENTY YEARS AGO IN 1350

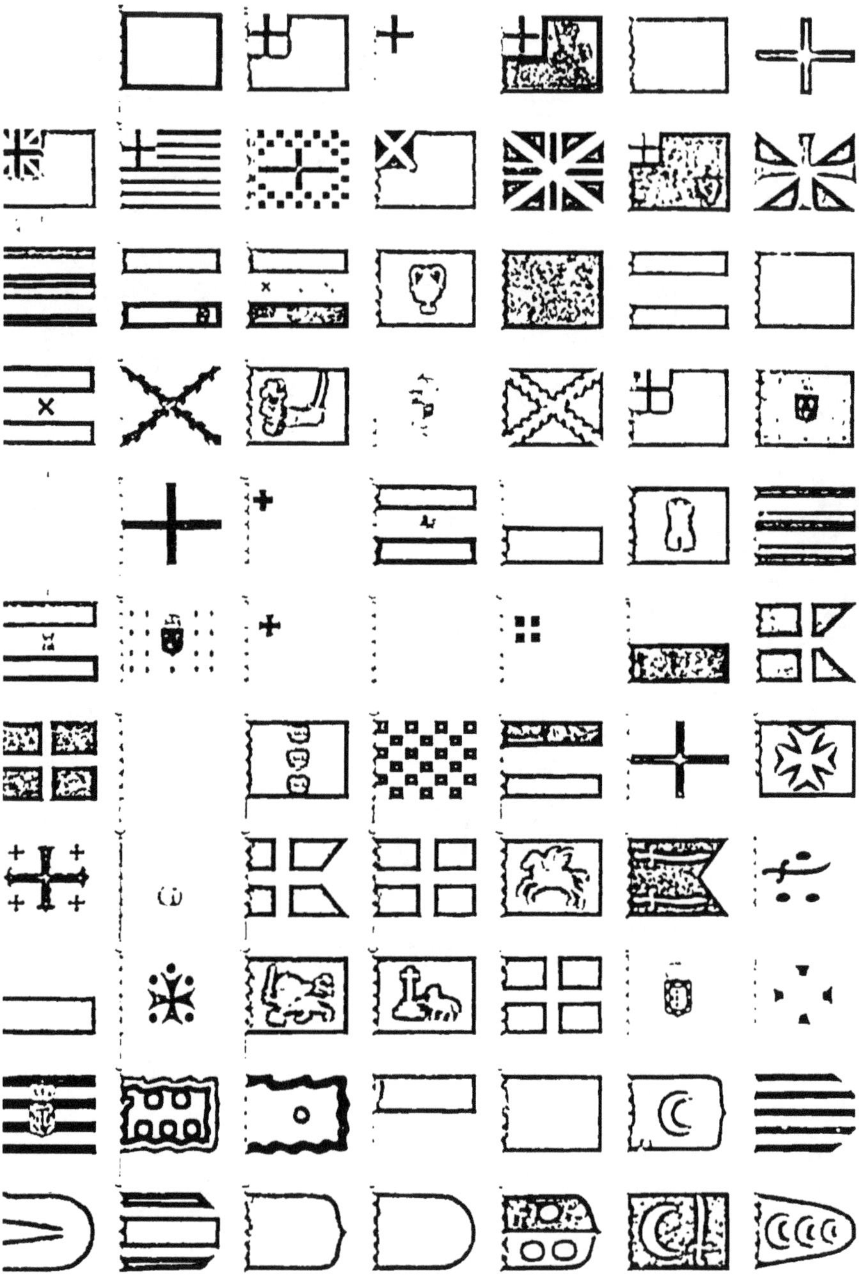

THE FLAGS OF EUROPE, ASIA, AND AFRICA

728. The flag of Abyssinia consists of three horizontal stripes, the uppermost green, the middle yellow, and the bottom red. This banner flies over that part of Africa which was known in Bible times as Ethiopia. It is the emblem of authority of a government which has been called a sort of feudal monarchy. The Emperor's title is "King of Kings." Certain parts of the country are ruled by princes, some of them appointed by the Emperor and others self-constituted. Some of these princes have retinues of supporters who are perpetual warriors and whose usefulness lasts as long as there are any insubordinate tribes to pacify. The Abyssinian army, numbering about 150,000, is largely composed of cavalry and is well adapted for swift movement, as it is not incumbered by any commissariat, its maintenance being obtained from the inhabitants of regions through which it passes.

729. The flag of Albania has a red field, upon which is imposed a black double-headed spread eagle. This flag dates from 1913, in which year a council of six members, chosen by the powers of Europe, set up the principality as an offset to Serbia's desire to possess a port on the Adriatic Sea. Austria resented Serbia's designs on the ground that the small nation would cut off the dual monarchy from an outlet to the Mediterranean in a way as prejudicial to her interests as the closed Dardanelles were prejudicial to the interests of Russia.

730. The coat-of-arms of Andorra, one of the four vest-pocket nations of the world, has a quartered shield bearing thereon the episcopal miter, the crozier of Urgel, the red and yellow pales of Aragon, and two belled cows. Andorra is under the joint sovereignty of France and the Spanish Bishop of Urgel. It is governed by a council of twenty-four members elected for four years by the heads of families in each parish. The council elects a first and second syndic to preside; the executive power is vested in the first syndic, while the judicial power is exercised by a civil judge and two magistrates. France and the Bishop of Urgel each appoint a magistrate and a civil judge alternately. The permanent delegate of the prefect of the Pyrenees-Orientales has charge of the interests of France in the republic.

731. A century ago Napoleon declared, "I recall a miniature republic lost in a corner of the Pyrenees." Today the hero, the conqueror, and the soldier, merely a handful of dust, is often recalled by Andorra. But in its mildness, its weakness, its isolation, the republic has found strength, and its colors float upon the breeze as independent as they were a century ago, when they waved over an island of peace in the great sea of human carnage during the Napoleonic wars. For nearly six centuries it has been thus. The war between France and England, begun at Crecy and Poitiers, did not move the tiny country. Queen Isabella and Ferdinand left it unmolested. Charles V, dreaming dreams of empire as great as those of Charlemagne, did not crush it upon his way to the Netherlands or to Italy. Philip II, weaving his web of expanding power around so many principalities, cast no entangling thread about it. Cynical Louis XI did not deign to harm it, and Louis XIV, although he ordered that there should be no more Pyrenees, left it undisturbed. It was a spectator of the Carlist War in Spain in 1833 and of the contest between France and Germany in 1870.

732. Built upon a rampart of rocks and hidden upon the southern slope of the Pyrenees, liberty has found a home in Andorra for a thousand years. Appreciating the services rendered by the Andorrans in his campaign against the Moors, Charlemagne gave them a charter of freedom and permitted them to govern themselves. Louis the Pious confirmed these rights, and from that day to this the tiny country has been self-governed under its own code of laws. The Spanish Bishop of Urgel holds spiritual supremacy and looks after educational matters and religious instruction. France exerts a temporal influence by appointing the provost from the department of Ariege to control the military activities of the republic. The blue, yellow, and red flag of Andorra, with its coronet in the center, is the youngest thing in the nation. It is only fifty years old, having originated in the reform of 1866 to emphasize the autonomy of the valley; but neither of the co-suzerains has approved it. It is displayed when the council is in session.

733. The flag of the Chinese army has a red field upon which is centered a black star bearing eight yellow points, with nine yellow disks on the body of the star. This is the flag of the republic and is entirely different from the one flown by the Chinese armies in the past.

734. The royal standard of Belgium consists of three vertical bars—black, yellow, and red—with black next the staff. The national arms are imposed upon the middle or yellow bar. These arms consist of a golden lion on a black ground. Its tongue and jaws are red. The shield is ensigned with the royal crown of Belgium and the supporters are two golden lions. The motto of Belgium is "L'Union fait la force" (Union makes strength). The black, yellow, and red of the Belgian flag are the colors of the Duchy of Brabant, and were adopted in 1831, when the monarchy was founded.

735. Belgium's merchant flag is a duplicate of the royal standard, except that the coat-of-arms is omitted.

736. The flag of the Chinese navy under the republic is red, with a blue canton in the upper corner next the staff, upon which is a large white sun with rays emanating in the form of small triangles. This flag succeeds the one in

blue and the apex half white. Upon the blue is placed a crowned anchor, proclaiming the government and the navy.

750. Italy's royal standard consists of a square blue field on which is centered the national coat-of-arms. A crown appears in each corner of the flag outside the encircling collar of the Annunciation. Within this collar is a crowned black spread-eagle on blue. On its breast is an oval shield bearing a silver cross on a red ground, the arms of Savoy (see also 1181). The collar itself is composed of a series of red and white roses and the letters F. E. R. T., meaning "Fortitudo ejus Rhodum tenuit" (His firmness held Rhodes), this being a tribute to Amadeus the Great from the Knights of St. John of Jerusalem, in 1310, for his help against the Saracens at the siege of Rhodes. The pendant of the collar of the Annunciation bears a design representing that holy event.

751. When Napoleon made the northern provinces of Italy into a kingdom, in 1805, he gave it a flag of three colors—green next to the flagstaff, white in the middle, and red at the fly end. This flag disappeared when Napoleon was overthrown, but was revived when Victor Emmanuel, King of Sardinia and a representative of the house of Savoy, became king. Today Italy's ensign consists of the Savoy arms, surmounted by a crown, on the central white vertical stripe of Napoleon's green, white, and red.

752. The Italian merchant flag is an exact duplicate of the ensign, with the exception that the crown is omitted above the arms.

753. The flag of the Governor of Eritrea, the Italian colony in Africa, consists of a white field upon which are imposed the arms and crown of Italy.

754. The flag of the Emperor of Japan consists of a red field upon which is centered a golden representation of the yellow chrysanthemum. It is essential that the flower should invariably have sixteen petals. While the use of this flower as a badge is not necessarily confined to the imperial family, its members alone have the right to use the sixteen-petalled form. If used by any other family, society, or corporation, it must be with a number of petals less or more than sixteen.

755. The flag of the Japanese crown prince is like that of the emperor, except that the chrysanthemum is centered in a rectangle formed by a line of white on the red field of the flag.

756. The Japanese ensign consists of a rising sun, slightly to the left of the center of a white field, with rays radiating to all points of the compass. Both the sun and the rays are red, and the device is generally known as the sunburst.

757. The Japanese merchant flag is white, of rectangular form, with a rayless red sun in the center, its diameter approximately half the width of the field.

758. The Japanese guard flag is of white, with two horizontal parallel dancetty lines in red across it. A "dancetty" line is zigzag, resembling the "worm" of a rail fence, with deep indentations.

759. The Japanese transport flag is identical with the Japanese guard flag, with the exception that the dancetty lines are blue instead of red.

760. The Japanese commanding officer's flag is a swallow-tail white, with the red sun and four rays, two vertical and two horizontal.

761. This flag, flown by all ships under Japanese registry carrying mail, consists of a white field with two horizontal red stripes, separated by a narrower white stripe occupying the upper half. The lower half is quartered by a red stripe, which, with the lower of the two horizontal red stripes, forms a T-square.

762. The flag which distinguishes a Japanese repair ship is the same as that displayed by a transport, with the exception that the bottom and top of the white field are bordered with red stripes.

763. In 1910 the Kingdom of Korea was abolished by Japan, whose influence in this territory had been recognized as paramount by the treaty which ended the Russo-Japanese War. The name of Chosen was given the State, and the red and white of the Japanese ensign were utilized in the flag adopted.

764. The national ensign of Liberia, which is also the merchant flag, has eleven horizontal stripes of red and white, red at the top and bottom, with the blue canton in the upper corner next to the flagstaff, on which is superimposed a large white star. This flag was adopted at the time the Republic of Liberia was established, in 1847, by colonists from America.

765. The flag of the President of Liberia consists of a square blue standard upon which is imposed a shield containing the red and white stripes of the national colors, and above it the five-pointed star of the republic.

766. The coat-of-arms of Liechtenstein (see 767) consists of a shield imposed upon the mantle of the Prince of the Holy Roman Empire, with his crown forming the crest. On the escutcheon, which is quartered, are the arms of Silesia for Ritberg; the second quarter of the shield, with its six stripes of red and gold, and green crown of rue cutting them diagonally, represents Khuenring; the third quarter, half red and half silver, is for Troppau; the fourth quarter, of gold, with its black harpy crowned, represents East Frisia. At the point of the shield in blue is a golden hunting horn, representing Jagerndorf; the small red and gold shield in the center, imposed upon all four quarters, represents Liechtenstein itself.

767. With its field shared by yellow and red, the latter occupying the lower half, the national banner of the principality of Liechtenstein flies over a nation having an area of 65 square miles. This miniature principality lies between Austria and Switzerland. It consists of Schellenberg and Vaduz, formerly fiefs of the Roman Empire. Schellenberg in 1699 and Vaduz in 1712 came into the possession of the House of Liechtenstein and were set up as a principality by Emperor Carl VI in 1719. After the break-up of the empire in 1806, the principality was incorporated in the Rhine Confederation. When the map of Europe was remade after the Napoleonic wars, it became a part of the German Confederation and remained so from that time until 1866, when the Confederation broke up. Since then it has not joined

782. Repair ships of the Netherlands fly a flag with the regulation red, white, and blue bars, the staff end of the red bar giving way to white and forming a canton upon which is placed a red anchor capped by a crown.

783. The royal standard of Norway has a red field upon which is centered a golden lion rampant holding a battle-ax.

784. Norway's ensign is red and three-tailed, a blue cross edged with white extending to a point between the swallow-tail. It thus preserves the shape of the Swedish ensign, from which it was fashioned, that ensign having a yellow cross on a blue field (see 826).

785 The merchant flag of Norway is like the ensign (784), except that the swallow-tail effect is omitted.

786. The senior admiral's flag of Norway consists of the ensign with the addition of a saltire cross of white in the upper quarter next to flagstaff.

787. The imperial standard of Persia consists of a blue square field with the national colors in a small canton in the upper corner next to the staff. In the center is a white circle on which the Persian coat-of-arms appears, showing a lion holding a sword, a rising sun in the background, and the crown of the empire above the lion. The lower half of the circle is bordered by a wreath.

788. The military flag of Persia is unique in that it embodies a very pale shade of green and a delicate shade of pink as the upper and lower hues of its tricolor. The middle stripe is white and bears the Persian sword-carrying lion with the sun peeping over his back. The crown of the empire is imposed upon the green stripe. The wreath rests upon the pink.

789. The ensign of Persia is like the military flag, except that the crown and wreath above and below the lion are omitted.

790. The merchant flag of Persia is the same green, white, and pink arrangement as seen in the ensign and military flag of the nation, but without the Persian lion.

791. The colors of the flag of Portugal are green and red, the third of the field next the staff green, and the two-thirds at the fly end red. The arms of the country are centered on the dividing line between the two colors. These arms consist of a large silver shield upon which are five small blue ones arranged in the form of a cross, each of them bearing five plates of silver. Around the shield is a red border upon which are placed seven golden castles. Alfonso I defeated five Moorish princes in the historic battle of Ourique and adopted the five small blue shields to commemorate his triumph. The five white spots on the small shields represent the five wounds of Christ, in whose strength Alfonso believed he had defeated the infidels. The red border of the shield was added by Alphonse III in 1252, after his marriage to a daughter of the King of Castile. The circle of gold upon which the shield and its border are imposed, together with the green of the flag, which is that of the cross and ribbon of the Knights of St. Benedict of Aviz, commemorate the fame of Prince Henry the Navigator.

792. The flag of the President of Portugal is solid green, with the Portuguese coat-of-arms in the center.

793. The flag of the Governor General of the provinces of Portugal is white, with a strip of green placed horizontally across the field and the coat-of-arms centered on it.

794. The flag of the dependent Kingdom of Poland (so nominated after the Napoleonic wars) has a white field with the blue cross of St. Andrew, which proclaims Russian suzerainty. Upon the red canton is a crowned spread eagle.

795. Roumania's flag has three vertical stripes, blue next the flagstaff, yellow in the middle, and red on the fly. In the standard the blue and the red bars are narrow and the yellow very wide. Upon the yellow is placed the national coat-of-arms, a canopy of ermine on which is a crowned shield. On the quartered field of the shield appear a golden eagle displayed on blue, a lion's head in gold displayed on red, a golden demilion issuing from an antique crown on red, and two dolphins in gold displayed on blue. There is also a small shield of pretense quartered in white and black. The shield is supported by golden lions rampant. The motto, "Nihil sine Deo" (Nothing without God), is below the shield on a ribbon. Four crowns appear, one in each corner of the flag.

796. The Roumanian ensign is like the standard, except that the three stripes are of equal width, and crowns in the four corners of the flag are omitted

797. Roumania's merchant flag is blue, yellow, and red, like the ensign, except that the arms are omitted.

798. The Roumanian coast guard flag has the national colors, together with an anchor, above which is a crown on the yellow stripe.

RUSSIAN FLAGS

799. The ensign of the Russian navy is a blue cross of St. Andrew upon a field of white. The Russians venerate St. Andrew as their patron saint, believing that it was he who secured the adoption of Christianity by their ancestors. It has been asserted that he preached in Scythia. Peter the Great, under his name and protection, in the year 1698, instituted St. Andrew's as the most noble order of Knighthood of the Empire. St. Andrew is also the patron saint of Scotland, but there the cross is white upon a field of blue (see 831).

800. The white, blue, and red horizontal stripes of the Russian merchant flag are reminiscent of the day when Peter the Great was learning ship-building in Holland. The Dutch flag is a tricolor of red, white, and blue. Peter, in making his flag, turned these colors upside down, but was afterward advised that he was flying the flag employed by the Dutch as a signal of distress and disaster. He thereupon revised his flag, putting the white at the top and the red at the bottom, with the blue between.

801. The flag of the volunteer fleet of Russia is the same as the merchant flag, except that there is a trumpet in the center of the blue field.

802. Russia's customs flag consists of a blue field with a canton in the upper corner next the staff showing the merchant flag in miniature, while in the lower corner next the staff are two combination caducei and tridents, crossed.

803

804

805

810

five stripes, three yellow and two red yellow at the top and bottom The central stripe is wider than the others The flag bears no device but the colors are those of Aragon and Castile

820 The flag of Switzerland consists of a red field with a white cross When the Red Cross was recognized at the International Conference at Geneva, in 1863, a distinguishing badge was devised for times of war and peace It will be noticed that the colors adopted are those of Switzerland counterchanged the red cross being in a white ground

821 The Captain General of the fleet of Spain flies the familiar red and yellow colors with an anchor placed horizontally on the yellow bar

822 Spanish ambassadors fly a swallow-tail flag made up of white red and yellow The third of the flag next to the staff is white and red white at the top and red below The middle bar of the flag is yellow and upon it two crossed tasseled pencils are imposed The third of the flag at the fly end is red

823 The flag of a Spanish minister is like that of an ambassador except that instead of the pencils there are three blue disks on the yellow bar

824 The military and naval service of Tunis has a flag consisting of a red field upon which is centered a white disk having a diameter half the vertical width of the flag Upon this disk a red crescent and a red star are imposed The flag is inherited from Turkey although it is no longer under Turkish domination

825 The royal standard of Sweden consists of a blue flag bearing a yellow cross This flag is swallowtailed and the horizontal arm of the cross in the fly projects Upon the intersection of the cross is placed the coat-of-arms of the country

826 The ensign of Sweden is like the royal standard, with the exception that the coat-of-arms is omitted

827 The merchant flag of Sweden is a rectangular blue flag bearing the yellow cross The blue and yellow were regarded as colors of freedom and independence at the time they were incorporated in the Swedish flag

828 The standard of the Bey of Tunis is a fearfully and wonderfully made flag It consists of seven horizontal stripes--red yellow, red green red yellow red the green stripe being double the width of the others The stripes do not extend the full length of the flag but join a narrow green stripe next to and parallel with the staff Every red stripe has four yellow-centered green disks and four yellow stars arranged alternately On every yellow stripe are four red stars and four black disks with red centers arranged in the same way On the broad central green stripe is a double-pointed dagger with white blade and red handle gold and red stars being distributed about it This flag is a western variation of the old flag of the days of Moslem authority In those days there were thirteen stripes instead of seven Tunis is now under French dominion and the tricolor is the supreme banner of the land

THE FLAGS OF THE BRITISH EMPIRE

829 The national flag of the British Empire, the union jack combines the crosses of St George (830) St Andrew (831) and St Patrick (832) When the union of the two crowns of England and Scotland took place upon the accession of James VI of Scotland to the English throne as James I the cross of St Andrew, the patron saint of Scotland and that of St George the patron saint of England were combined and all ships were ordered to fly at their maintop the new flag, while at the foretop the English were still to fly the red cross of St George and the Scots the white cross of St Andrew

This was the first union jack (361) as it is generally termed though strictly speaking the name of the flag is 'great union,' being a jack only when flown from the jackstaff of a ship of war James I always signed his name "Jacques" and it is believed in many quarters that the jack and the jackstaff of the navy derived their names from that fact Others contend that 'jack' was used as early as the close of the sixteenth century Lord Howard's ships in their attack upon the Spanish Armada in 1588 are described as carrying a "jack" on the jackstaff, their jack being a small edition of the red cross of St George

That St George's cross was placed over St Andrew's was distressing to the Scots, who made it the subject of an appeal to the King (see 1132) But even a king cannot solve all of the problems of heraldry That art has no way of making two devices on a flag of equal value If they be put side by side the position next the staff is more honorable than the one remote from it just as the upper portion of a flag is more honorable than the lower After the death of Charles I the union of Scotland and England was dissolved and the ships of parliament reverted to the use of the simple cross of St George while those of Scotland took up the cross of St Andrew again When Cromwell became protector he restored the union flag, imposing the Irish harp upon its center

After the Restoration, Charles II removed the harp, and so the original union flag was revived and continued in that form until 1801, when upon the legislative union of Great Britain and Ireland the cross of St Patrick was incorporated To combine these crosses without losing the characteristic features of each was not easy Each had to be distinct and at the same time retain a border which would denote its original ground To place the red cross of St Patrick on the white cross of St Andrew would have obliterated the latter and *vice versa* Therefore it was decided to make the white broader on one side of the red than

830

831

nexed the English, and felt so bitter about it that for many years after the union on all shields devoted to Scottish business, and on the flag displayed north of the Tweed, the arms of Scotland were placed in the first quarter, as they are on the monument to Queen Elizabeth in Westminster Abbey (see also 1132).

The early standard of Ireland contained three gold crowns on a blue field. Henry VIII substituted the harp, and James I finally placed it on the third quarter of the royal standard. The Earl of Northampton, writing in the reign of King James I, suggested that the best reason that he could observe for the use of the harp was that it resembled the country it typified in being "an instrument that cost more to keep it in tune than it was worth."

The royal standard is hoisted only when the King is actually within the palace or castle, or at the saluting point, or on board the vessel which flies it. The King's regulations say: "The royal standard, being the personal flag of a sovereign, is not to be displayed in future on board His Majesty's ship or on general buildings, as has hitherto been customary, on His Majesty's birthday and other occasions, but it shall only be hoisted on occasions when the sovereign is actually present, or when any member of the royal family is present representing the sovereign."

834. The white ensign, bearing the red cross of St George, with the union jag of the Empire in its canton, is the fighting flag of the Royal Navy. When at anchor in home ports the British ships hoist their colors at 8 o'clock in the morning in the summer, and at 9 o'clock in the winter; and when abroad, either at 8 or 9, as the commander-in-chief directs. On the hoisting of the ensign all work stops and all ranks must get on deck, standing at the salute as the band plays the opening bars of the national anthem, the man at the halyards timing his pulls so that the ensign reaches the truck at the last note of the band, just as it reaches the deck in the evening when it is hauled down. The regulations provide that British ships shall not on any account lower their flags to any foreign ships whatsoever, unless the foreign ships shall first, or at the same time, lower their flags to them.

835. The blue ensign of the British Empire is now flown by naval reserve vessels, public offices about the consular service, the government vessels of the several colonies, by hired transports, by hired surveying vessels commanded by officers of the royal navy, by commissioned officers serving as mail agents, by the Fishery Board for Scotland, by the Pacific Cable Board ships, by Lloyds (on boats), by the Indian Marine, and by Royal Naval Reserve. The privilege of flying the blue ensign is also allowed to British merchantmen commanded by officers on the retired list of the royal navy, or by officers of the Royal Naval Reserve, on condition that either officer commanding the ship is one of these, that ten of the crew belong to the reserve, or that the ship is in receipt of an admiralty warrant. Yacht clubs (except the royal, which flies the white) fly the blue ensign. When flown by ships belonging to the British public service, it bears in the fly the seal or badge of the office to which the ship is accredited. For example, hired transports fly it with a yellow anchor in the fly (see 846); the ordnance department of the War Office displays it with a shield on the fly bearing a cannon and cannon balls (see 854).

836. No other flag in the world flutters in the breeze of as many ports or sails as far and wide as the red ensign of the British Merchant Marine. At the beginning of the present war nearly one half of all of the cargo- and passenger-carrying ships of the earth sailed under these colors. It is not improbable that more than half of all the passengers and cargoes sailing the seven seas were carried upon them, for no nation's ships were more efficiently handled. At that time the tonnage of the British Merchant Marine was more than four times as great as that of Germany.

837. Uther Pendragon, father of King Arthur, had a vision of a flaming dragon in the sky. This his seers interpreted as meaning that he should ascend the throne. After his accession he had two golden dragons fashioned, one of which he carried into battle. The Anglo-Saxon kings were impressed with the image, and incorporated it into their arms. Not until the twentieth century was it officially restored as proper only to the race of Uther Pendragon. Under the reign of Edward VII it was incorporated into the armorial bearing of the Prince of Wales.

838. The lion rampant with the tressure, which is the device of Scotland, and which is seen in the second quarter of the British royal standard, first appeared on the seal of King Alexander II about 1230 A. D. Without modification in color or form it was borne by all the sovereigns of Scotland, and on the accession of James VI to the throne of England as James I, in the year 1603, it became an integral part of the King's standard, and has so remained to this day.

839. The story of the harp of Ireland which appears on the blue field of the Irish standard has been told in the account of the history of the British royal standard (833), on which it appears in the third quarter (see also 1133).

840. The three golden lions of the standard of England are, as told in 833, of doubtful origin. Certain it is that, except for the break which occurred in the years that Cromwell was Protector, they have typified the might of England for seven hundred years.

841. The royal family's standard of the British Empire is the same as the royal standard (833), except that it has a white border and bears as an escutcheon of pretence the arms of Saxony (658), proclaiming the continental origin of the royal family. As the name of the reigning family has been changed recently, it is probable also that its standard will be changed in this same particular.

842. The flag of the Lord Lieutenant of Ireland is the national flag of the British Empire, with the golden harp of the Irish on a blue escutcheon at the intersection of the crosses.

843. The County Lords Lieutenant, when on land, fly the union with a crown over a sword borne horizontally along the middle arm of St George's cross. Each county of Great Britain and Ireland has such a chief official

881. A large and two small ships within a garter surmounted by a crown constitute the principal device of the badge of the Bahamas. On the garter are words which tell us that the pirates have been expelled and that business has been resumed. This is the badge of the group of islands which include what is now known as Watling's Island, believed to have been the first landing place of Christopher Columbus, who called it San Salvador.

882. The badge of Sombrero and Bahama Lights has a blue field bearing a ring of red inclosing a lighthouse shedding its rays. The ring is crowned and inscribed "Board of Trade." Above the crown is a scroll bearing the word "Bahamas."

883. Jamaica's badge shows an escutcheon bearing St. George's cross and surmounted by a lizard. Upon the cross are distributed, one at each arm and one at the intersection, five pineapples. The escutcheon is supported by two Indians.

884. The Turks and Caicos Islands, which are close to the Bahamas, have an escutcheon which consists of a full-rigged sailing ship in the background, a man making salt in the middle foreground, and the name of the islands below.

885. On the badge of the Leeward Islands appears in the middle distance a mountainous coast, skirted by a full-rigged ship; in the foreground is another ship; on the shore a pineapple, larger than either ship, and three smaller ones. Above the whole appear the British royal arms.

886. Britannia, robed in blue, red, and ermine, and ruling the waves from the backs of two sea-horses, forms the principal scheme of the badge of Barbados. One sea-horse in this badge has a blue tail.

887. The Windward Isles have a badge which makes use of a garter encircling a blue field, upon which is placed a quartered shield—red, yellow, green, and purple. The device is crowned. The motto is, "I, Pede Fausto," "Make a propitious beginning."

888. St. Lucia, the chief coaling station of the British fleet in the West Indies, has for a badge a landscape in which appear the Pitons, twin mountains of the island, and the ever-bubbling volcano Soufrière, with a land-locked harbor in the foreground. The Latin motto below describes this harbor as "Hardly a faithless guard for ships."

889. St. Vincent's badge has a classical group showing a woman holding a branch and another kneeling before the altar of the law, upon which she is placing a wreath. The badge bears the motto, "Pax et Justicia."

890. Discovered by Columbus on his third voyage, Grenada seems to have taken his ship, in full sail and running before a spanking breeze toward the island, as its badge. The inscription "Clarior e Tenebris" means "Brighter out of the darkness," and doubtless refers to the fact that Grenada is beyond the hurricane line.

891. The badge of British Guiana, the British Empire's continental holdings on the coast of South America, consists of a clipper in full sail surrounded by a garter of gold.

892. The facts that British Honduras is a mahogany colony, that it belongs to the British Empire, and that it is given to trading, are brought out in the shield of the colony, which is circular, one-third of it being devoted to the display of the tools of mahogany logging, the second third showing the union jack, while the remaining third bears a full-rigged sailing ship.

893. Trinidad and Tobago have a badge which shows a mountain in the background, a frigate in the left middle ground, and a blue ensign on a jetty in the right middle ground. A boat, a smaller ship, a house, and several spars showing behind the jetty complete the picture. Below, on white, is a Latin inscription meaning "He approves of the people uniting and entering into treaties."

894. A white bull standing in tussac grass and a frigate in a river close by form the badge of the Falkland Islands, lying off South America and belonging to England.

895. The smaller British islands of the Pacific are under the control of the Western Pacific High Commissioner. His badge is the crown of the Empire above the letters W P H C.

896. The main feature of the badge of the Fiji Islands is an escutcheon bearing at the top on red the British lion. Below is the red cross of St. George on white. The quarters thus formed bear specimens of the vegetable and bird life of the islands. The shield is supported by two Polynesians wearing skirts of straw and standing on a scroll upon which is inscribed a motto in the native language. The crest is a native catamaran in full sail.

897. The resident commissioner of the New Hebrides has as a badge a disk of white encircled by a wreath of green and red and bearing a crown with the words NEW HEBRIDES around it.

898. The Protectorate of the British Solomon Islands has a simple badge, consisting of the royal crown, surrounded by the three words on a white field, BRITISH SOLOMON ISLANDS.

899. The British Resident of the Gilbert and Ellice Islands, in the southern Pacific, has a badge which consists of a white field bearing below the letters B R, above which is a crown.

900. The Governor of New Zealand flies a flag which consists of the national flag of the British Empire, bearing at the intersection of the crosses the badge of the island (901).

901. New Zealand's badge is a wreath-encircled design of white, bearing four stars in the form of a cross, with the letters N Z in the center. The stars are emblematic of the southern cross, which appears in the skies over New Zealand.

902. The blue ensign of New Zealand bears the southern cross on the fly, the stars being red with white borders.

903. The red ensign of New Zealand bears the southern cross in white stars of five points.

904. The ensign of Paratonga, which flies over sundry islands in the Pacific, has a field consisting of three stripes, the upper and the lower red and the middle one white. Upon the white stripe are three five-pointed blue stars.

905 [illegible]

906 [illegible]

907 [illegible]

908 [illegible]

909 [illegible]

910 [illegible]

911 [illegible]

912 [illegible]

913 [illegible]

914 [illegible]

926 Hongkong's badge shows a harbor scene in which appear a junk and a tea clipper. Hongkong is a Chinese city now under British sovereignty, and possessed of a naval base of first magnitude.

927 Weihaiwei, a British holding on the Chinese coast, is represented by a badge upon which appear two mandarin ducks on the banks of a stream.

928 The motto of Mauritius proclaims it "The star and the key of the Indian Seas." On its badge, which is a quartered shield, azure and gold, appear the symbolical key and star and a galley. The supporters are a red and white dodo on the dexter side and a red and white antelope on the sinister. Each of the supporters has a stalk of sugar cane in front of it. Mauritius is an island in the Indian Ocean, 500 miles from Madagascar, having about 720 square miles of territory and about 377,000 inhabitants.

929 Seychelles and its dependencies consist of ninety islands and islets, with a total estimated area of 150 square miles, lying along the coast of Africa. They are represented on its badge by a tall palm tree, with a smaller tree near by and a turtle at its foot, and the motto *Finis coronat opus*.

930 The ensign of the Federated Malay States is one of the comparatively few ensigns of the world that use black. The field consists of four horizontal stripes, white at the top, then red, yellow, and black in order. Upon the center is an oval of white bearing a running tiger. The Federated Malay States are Perak, Selangor, Negri-Sembilan, and Pahang. They occupy a large portion of the Malay peninsula and are under British protection.

931 The jack of the Federated Malay States has a unique design. It preserves the colors of the Malay States ensign, but uses them as triangles instead of stripes. The red triangle has its base on the staff; the black triangle, its base on the fly; the base of the white triangle is at the upper edge, and that of the yellow at the bottom. The apexes of the triangles meet in the center of the flag.

932 The ensign of Pahang, one of the four Federated Malay States, has a field the upper half of which is white and the lower half black. Pahang has 14,000 square miles of territory and a population of 118,000.

933 The ensign of Negri-Sembilan, one of the four Federated Malay States, consists of a yellow field with a union bearing two triangles, one of which, its base resting on the staff, is black, and the other, its base resting on the yellow field, is red.

934 Perak, also a Federated Malay State, has an ensign consisting of three horizontal stripes, the upper white, the lower black, and the middle yellow.

935 The ensign of Selangor is yellow and red and is quartered. The first quarter is red and bears the star and crescent of the Mohammedan world; the second quarter is yellow, the third yellow, and the fourth red. Selangor is about the size of Delaware and has a population of 300,000.

936-945 (inclusive). These are the flags of the Malay States not included in the Federation. They are all under British protection. The relations of Johore with Great Britain are defined by a treaty dated December 11, 1885, amended by agreement on May 12, 1914, in which the Sultan agreed to accept and to act upon the advice of a British officer called the general adviser. The rights of suzerainty, protection, administration, and control of the other four States were transferred from Siam to Great Britain by the Anglo-Siamese treaty of March 10, 1909. The State of Kelantan, on the east coast of the peninsula, with an area of 5,870 square miles and a population approximating 300,000, is represented by 936 and 937, ensign and merchant flags respectively. There are only four post-offices in the entire State. The flag of Johore (938) is black, with a red union bearing the star and crescent of the Mohammedan religion. The flag of the Sultan of Johore (939) is white, bearing a crescent and star in blue, the star being nine-pointed. Perlis flies a yellow and black flag (940), the upper half yellow and the lower black. The Rajah of Perlis flies a yellow flag (941) with a shield inclosed within a wreath. The flag of Kedah (942) is red, with a green crescent and a shield half surrounded by a wreath. That of the Sultan of Kedah (943) is yellow, with a green shield, a red crescent, and a green wreath. The Regent of Kedah flies a green flag (944) bearing a yellow shield, crescent, and wreath. Trengganu has a flag (945) the staff third of which is white and the remainder black.

946 The Governor General of India flies the familiar union jack with the star of India, crowned, at the intersection of the crosses.

947 The badge of India consists of a five-pointed star inclosed within a garter and surrounded by golden rays, as a sunflower. Above is the crown of the Empire.

948 The Indian marine flies the blue ensign of Great Britain with the star of India in the fly.

949 The jack of the Indian marine is the union jack on a field of blue.

950 The flag of the local Indian maritime government is the blue ensign of Britain bearing on the fly a golden lion rampant carrying in its forepaws the crown of Empire.

951 The flag of the Conservators of Bombay has seven horizontal red stripes separated by thin white stripes. The central red stripe forms with a perpendicular bar the red cross of St George, on which is centered the seal of the Conservators, consisting of two small escutcheons leaning together on a field of white and having a crown above them.

952 The flag of the Trustees of Bombay, a body which has in charge the light-houses and other shipping activities on the Bombay coast, has a blue cross placed on the field corresponding to the red cross of St George. This cross quarters the field, the first quarter bearing a light-house, the light represented by rays of red, and the other three quarters bear shipping scenes along the coast.

953 The Witu forest lies within the protectorate of British East Africa. Its flag is a red field upon which is centered a union jack, about half as long and half as wide as the field itself.

954 British ascendency in Egypt dates from the 18th of December, 1914, when the govern-

FLAGS OF AUSTRIA-HUNGARY, BULGARIA, GERMANY, AND TURKEY

987. The ensign of Austria-Hungary has three horizontal stripes, red at the top and bottom, with white between. Upon the white stripe are imposed the shield of Austria next the staff and of Hungary next the fly. Above each shield is the crown of its kingdom. The Hungarian crown differs from the Austrian, being that of St. Stephen. The Austrian shield repeats the red, white, red-striped design of the flag, and was the device of the ancient dukes of Austria, dating back to the twelfth century.

988. The merchant flag of Austria-Hungary was introduced in 1869 by a commission appointed to blend the flags of the two countries. As the Hungarian flag is red, white, and green, the blending was accomplished by making the bottom stripe of the Austro-Hungarian ensign one-half green. Thus the half of the merchant flag containing the Hungarian shield preserves the distinctive Hungarian tricolor.

989. The imperial standard of Austria-Hungary consists of a yellow field bordered with small black, red, and white triangles representing flames. It is square and in the center are placed the arms of the Austrian monarchy. These consist of a black double-headed eagle crowned, the double head indicating the former Holy Roman Empire. Over the eagle appears the crown of Austria. In one claw the eagle holds a sword and scepter and in the other an orb. On its breast appears a shield divided equally into three vertical portions. The red lion rampant on a golden ground in the first section represents the House of Hapsburg; the silver section on a red ground stands for Austria; the three eaglets in silver on a red band upon a golden ground are reminiscent of Lorraine. The shield is surrounded by the colors of the Order of the Golden Fleece and of Maria Theresa. On the wings of the eagle are the arms of the eleven provinces. This flag commands a different salute from any other in the world, it is believed. Under Austrian naval usage the Emperor is saluted by twenty-one guns followed by fifteen hurrahs. A minister of state or field marshal gets nineteen guns and eleven hurrahs; a general thirteen guns and seven hurrahs; a commodore eleven guns and three hurrahs, while ambassadors, archbishops, consuls, and others all have their definite share of gunpowder and requisite allotment of shouting.

990. The royal standard of Bulgaria is a square red flag bordered with black and green triangles, upon which is emblazoned the royal lion of the coat-of-arms of the country. On the body of the lion is a shield having a blue field bearing a series of diagonal and horizontal lines.

991. The ensign of Bulgaria is white at the top, red at the bottom, and green between. In a canton appears the golden lion rampant of the Bulgarian arms, upon red. The lion is crowned.

992. Bulgaria's merchant flag is of white, green, and red, white at the top and red at the bottom.

993. Germany's imperial standard has a cross, black with white border, the field being yellow, and the intersection of the cross bearing a shield containing the arms of Prussia surmounted by a crown and surrounded by the collar of the Order of the Black Eagle. The yellow field of the flag is diapered over in each corner with three black eagles and the crown. The arms of the cross reach out to the four edges of the flag and bear the legend, "Gott Mit Uns, 1870," the date commemorating the origin of this standard.

994. The standard of the King of Prussia very closely resembles the imperial standard, except that the field of the flag is red instead of yellow. The cross which this flag and the preceding one bear is the cross of the Teutonic order and dates from the close of the twelfth century.

995. The ensign of the German Empire has a white field, upon which is imposed a large black cross, having at its center a circle in black outlines containing the black Prussian eagle crowned. The arms of the cross quarter the flag. In the canton there is the merchant flag in miniature, upon which is superimposed the black cross of the Teutonic order (994).

996. The merchant flag of Germany, consisting of three bars, black at the top, white in the middle, and red at the bottom, dates from 1867. In that year it was decreed that the flag of the North German Confederacy should be black, white, and red, and when the twelve southern States joined the federation the same flag was continued as the merchant symbol of the Empire. Prior to 1867 no German national flag had ever flown upon the ocean, each of the various States and free cities having its own special colors (see also 1153, 1154, 1166, etc.). In a speech delivered that year the Minister of the Crown stated that the combination of colors was emblematic of a junction of the black and white Prussian flag with the red and white ensign of the Hanseatic League.

997. The standard of the King of Bavaria has a field of blue and white lozenges, upon which is centered the coat-of-arms of the kingdom. This bears a quartered shield with a golden lion, crowned, on a field of black, representing the Rhine Palatinate in the first quarter; the second quarter is red and silver for the Duchy of Franconia; the third quarter has eight stripes of silver and red crossed by a pale of gold, for the Margravate of Burgau; the fourth quarter has a blue lion rampant, crowned with gold, for the County of Veldentz. Upon all is a fusiform of striped silver and blue, which represents Bavaria. Above this

998

999

1000

1001

1002

1003

1004

1005

1006

1007

1008

1009

1010

1019 The chief of the staff of the German navy flies a flag of white, [illegible] quartered by a black cross, upon whose intersection is imposed a disk of white [illegible] gold [illegible] and a sword.

1020 The [illegible] of the German navy consists of a swallow-tailed pennant hung free from the flagstaff and bearing a black cross.

1021 The Sultan of Turkey flies a different flag [illegible] from that which is borne [illegible]. As commander-in-chief of the Turkish naval forces he [illegible] banner upon which is centered [illegible] white [illegible] with [illegible] star in the center of each quarter of the flag.

1022 The [illegible] flag of Turkey is green [illegible] of the [illegible] banner [illegible] the usual crescent [illegible] white [illegible] that is borne upon all religious occasions. It has been under this banner that untold thousands of Christians in the Mohammedan world have suffered at the hands of the followers of Islam.

1023 The customs [illegible] of Turkey is of the same general design as the national ensign, except that the star and crescent are inclosed in a rectangle [illegible] white stripe close to and parallel with the border.

1024 The [illegible] Crete is quartered by a white cross. The first quarter is red and bears a five-pointed star in white, while the other three quarters are blue. This was the flag of the [illegible] commissioner appointed by Great Britain, Russia, France, and Italy, and later proposed by Greece with the permission of the Powers [illegible] the island before its annexation to Greece.

HEROIC FLAGS OF THE MIDDLE AGES

[illegible] Historic Standards

(Nos. 1025-1120)

THE earliest representation of the flags of [illegible] is to be found in an illuminated manuscript of a Franciscan friar, a native of Spain, who was born in 1305, and who, according to his own claim, wrote his monumental "Book of the Knowledge of All the Kingdoms, Countries, and Lordships that there are in the World, and of the Ensigns and Arms of Each Country and Lordship; also of the Kings and Lords Who Govern Them," after having visited all the places which he describes.

Geographers and historians hesitate to accept the friar's claim as literally true, but it is evident that he was a great traveler and a close observer; and though he is prone to weave legend and hearsay into his narrative, there is nevertheless a remarkable fund of information in this priceless manuscript, written a century and a half before Columbus discovered America, and which now reposes in the Biblioteca Nacional at Madrid.

[illegible] AS WELL AS [illegible]

The manuscript of the anonymous Franciscan whose travels extended as far east as Java, by way of Mecca, was edited by the Spanish scholar Marcos Jiménez de la Espada 30 years ago, with the aid of Don Francisco Coello, the eminent geographer. It was recently published in English, together with the flags (see page 371), by the Hakluyt Society.

The devices are very beautiful and rich, both in color and in design, the Franciscan evincing great skill in reproducing in some instances the banners and in others the coats-of-arms of the kingdoms and principalities which he visited.

The story of these flags of the world 570 years ago and of the kings and countries over which they waved is best told in the words of the Franciscan himself, who makes no attempt to differentiate between what he actually saw and what he heard (the numbers in the text refer to the corresponding flag on page 371):

[illegible] God the Father and Son and Holy Ghost, three individual persons in [illegible] I was born in the Kingdom of Castile, in the reign of the very noble King [illegible] [illegible] Hebrews [illegible] years, and [illegible] 4,907 years [illegible] Nabu[illegible] [illegible] Christ 1,304 years, and of the Arabs 706, on the 11th day of the month of September.

There are in the Kingdom of Castile 28 cities and many other towns, castles, and villages. Know that this Kingdom of Castile and Leon has all the sea [illegible] of [illegible] Navarre and Aragon and Granada. The ensigns of the kings of this kingdom are a flag with two castles and two lions quartered (1025).

I departed from the [illegible]

[illegible] western [illegible] and the [illegible] (1026)

[illegible] (1027)

[illegible]

(1028)

[illegible] (1029)

[illegible]

(1030)

[illegible] (1031)

[illegible]

board a ship, I passed to an island they called Gotlandia, which is in the German Gulf, and on this island there is a great city called Bisuy (Wisby), in which there are 90 parishes, and the island is well peopled. There is a smaller island called Oxilia. The king of these islands has a flag of gold and purple bars" **(1039)**.

It was in the century preceding the Franciscan's visit that the wealth of the city of Wisby, or Bisuy, as he called it, became proverbial, and an old ballad relates that "the Gotlanders weigh gold with 20-pound weights and play with the choicest gems. The pigs eat out of silver troughs and the women spin with gold distaffs. A few years after the friar's visit Wisby was attacked by the King of Denmark, who after a bloody battle, in which 1,800 peasants fell trying to defend the gates of the city, took possession of the whole island.

"I ascended the lofty mountains of Noruega (Norway), which is a very strong kingdom containing three great cities. They call the largest Regis (Bergen), where they crown the kings. And be it known that this Noruega toward the north is uninhabited, and that the year makes one day for six months and another six months' night, and there are men who have their heads fixed on their breasts with no neck whatever, but I did not see them. The king of this Noruega has for his device a flag—gold with a black lion **(1040)**.

"I departed from Noruega in a ship of the English, and we shaped a course west and came to an island, very large, called Salanda, which is at the entrance of the Gulf of Frisia, already mentioned. The island of Salanda (Zeeland) is very populous and has four great cities, called Salandi (Copenhagen), Risent (Ringsted), Escondin (Stor Hedding), Alenda (Lealand). The king of this island has for his device a flag—gold with a black lion, as in Noruega **(1040)**.

"I left the island of Salanda (Zeeland) and we made a long voyage, arriving at another island called Tille (Telemarken, in the south of Norway), and from thence we came to the island of Escocia (Scotland) and found in it three great cities—one called Donfres (Dumfries), another Eneruic (Edinburgh), another Veruic (Berwick). The king of this Escocia has for his device a red flag with three long lions of gold" **(1041)**.

The explanation for the Franciscan's confusion of the arms of England with those of Scotland is quite simple. His visit took place during the reign of David Bruce, who married an English princess, and he probably saw her arms on a flag in Scotland and assumed it to be the device of the reigning monarch.

ENGLAND CONTAINED "ELEVEN GREAT CITIES"

"I departed from the land of Escocia and came to the Kingdom of Inglaterra (England). Know that it is a very well populated country and that it contains eleven great cities. The largest, where they crown their king, is called Londres (London). The king of those lands has for his arms, on a flag quarterly, in two quarters, fleurs de lys, gold on a field azure, because the king is of the house of France, and in the other two quarters, in each one, on a field gules (red), three ounces gold" **(1042)**.

The "ounces" which the friar depicts in his device for the English king, it will be observed, are almost identical with the "long lions" which he erroneously credited to Scotland **(1041)**.

"I left Inglaterra in a boat and reached the island of Irlanda (Ireland), which is a short crossing of a mile (!). They say that formerly it was called Ibernia. In this island there is a great lake, and they say that the lake brings good fortune, because many enchantments were made on its bank in ancient times. The king of this island has the same arms as the King of Inglaterra **(1042)**.

"Being in Irlanda, I sailed in a ship bound for Spain, and went with those on that ship on the high sea for so long that we arrived at the island of Eterns (Faroe Islands), and another called Artania (Orkneys), and another called Citilant (Shetland Islands), and another called Ibernia (Iceland). All these islands are in a part where the sun (never?) sets in the month of June and they are all peopled. In Ibernia there are trees and the fruit that they bear are very fat birds. These birds are very good eating, whether boiled or roasted. The men in this island are very long lived, some living 200 years. They are born and brought up in a way which makes them unable to die in the islands, so that when they become very weak they are taken away and die presently.

"In this island there are no snakes nor vipers, nor toads, nor flies, nor spiders, nor any other venomous things, and the women are very beautiful, though very simple. It is a land where there is not as much bread as you may want, but a great abundance of meat and milk. The king of this island has for his device the same flag as the King of Noruega **(1040)**.

"After this I departed from the island of Ibernia in a ship, and voyaged so far over the western sea that we sighted Cape Finisterre and arrived at Pontevedra, in the province of Galicia (Spain). Thence I went to a town in the Kingdom of Castile, as I mentioned before, which they call Tarifa. It was founded by a very powerful Arab named Tarif. Near this town Albuacen, king of all the land of the west, was defeated and conquered by the very noble king, Don Alfonso of Castile, who pillaged all his tents and took his treasures, his women, and his horses." (This was the battle of Salado, in which the King of Castile, Alfonso XI, defeated Abu-l-hasan Ali, King of Morocco, on October 28, 1340.)

"I departed from Tarifa and went to the city of Aljezira (Algeciras), where is the rock of Gibraltar, being places in the dominions of the King of Castile.

"I went to Malaga, a very luxurious city of the Kingdom of Granada. In this kingdom there are three cities. The grandest, where they crown the kings, is Granada. This kingdom is bounded by the Mediterranean and the Kingdom of Castile. The device of this king is a red flag with Arabic letters of gold, such as Mahomad, their prophet, bore" **(1043)**.

The friar made an altogether excusable error in copying the Arabic inscription, which should read, "No conqueror but God."

"I departed from the Kingdom of Granada

The Knights of the Order of the Hospital of St. John of Jerusalem, afterward known as the Knights of Rhodes and the Sovereign Order of the Knights of Malta, came into existence in Jerusalem during the First Crusade. After its expulsion from the Holy Land at the fall of the Latin Kingdom, the order was established in Rhodes in 1309, where it was holding sway at the time of the friar's visit and where it remained until 1522.

"I left the island of Rhodes and went to the island of Candia (Crete), and thence to another island they call Negropont (Eubœa), which the Venetians conquered. I left the entrance to the greater sea and Constantinople, which I will describe further on, to my left, and went to the city they call Satalia (Adalia), of Greek Christians. This Satalia is part of the province of Naturi (Anatolia). The King of this Satalia has for his device a flag with bars wavy argent and purpure and over all the sign of Solomon's seal" **(1059)**.

Adalia, known in ancient times as Attalia, played a conspicuous part in the history of the eastern Mediterranean during the Middle Ages. It was from this port that Louis VII sailed for Syria in 1148, and it was the assembling point for Richard Cœur de Lion's descent upon Cyprus during the Third Crusade.

THE RICH LAND OF TURKEY

"The city of Satalia and others as far as the lesser Armenia are all in the province of Turquia (Turkey), which was called, in ancient times, Asia Minor. In it there are many lordships and provinces which it would be hard to enumerate, for this Turquia extends to the greater sea, and be it known that it is a very rich land, well supplied with all goods. The king of this province has this flag for his device **(1060)**.

"I went along the coast of this Turquia to a city called Corincho (Kongos). The king of this land has a black flag with five white crosses **(1061)**.

"I departed from Corincho and went to the city they call Feradelfia, or Feradelfin (Philadelphia), which marches on that of Troy, which in ancient times King Menelaus of Greece destroyed. Troy was the head of all that Asia Minor which they now call Turquia, and its device is a flag half white, with a red cross, the other half yellow, with a red square **(1063)**.

"In this Turquia there is another province they call Cunio (Iconium, modern Konia), in which there is a rich city called Cunyo, with much territory, and the king has a flag with bars wavy argent and gules" **(1064)** (silver and red).

Following its conquest by the Seljuk Turks in the eleventh century, Konia became one of the most brilliant cities of the medieval world. Many splendid mosques, palaces, and tombs adorned the place, which was surrounded by a wall two miles in circumference. Beyond the city proper spread the gardens and villas of a numerous suburban population. From the splendor of the city sprang the Turkish proverb, "See all the world, but see Konia."

"There is also another province called Sauasto (Sebastia, or Siwas), anciently Sausco, from a city of that name which was the head of all the cities. This city of Sauasco was the ancient Samaria, though now it is Sauasco, head of the kingdom, with a white flag having five red crosses **(1064)**.

In the time of the Franciscan Siwas, known in ancient times as Megalopolis-Sebastia, was enjoying its second period of prosperity, having been rebuilt by the great Sultan Ala-eddin Kaikobad I. Fifty years after the friar wrote his "Knowledge of the World," Siwas' flag was trampled in the dust by the implacably cruel Tamerlane, who buried alive 4,000 of its inhabitants.

"I entered Armenia the Less, which is all surrounded by very high mountains, and within the mountains there is a plain country in which there are 360 towns and villages and castles."

This reference should not be confused with the Armenia of today. The Franciscan is referring to a small principality founded in 1080, which gradually grew until it became the independent kingdom of Lesser Armenia. It was a Christian State set in the midst of Moslem principalities and gave valuable assistance to the Crusaders, although it was hostile to the Byzantine rulers. It had a tempestuous existence extending over a period of about three centuries.

"On the shores of the Mediterranean Sea, in the place where it ends, you must know that anciently this Armenia was called the island of Colcos; for in this Armenia an arm of the sea enters in which there is a small island called Porto Bonel (in the Gulf of Alexandretta, or Iskanderun), and here was the temple to the enchanted golden sheep which bewitched Jason the Greek.

"After this Armenia is the island of Chipre (Cyprus), and in this Chipre there are four great cities. The King of Chipre has for his design a flag parted per pale argent five crosses gules and purpure (purple), two fleurs de lys palewise, because he is of the House of France" (Armenia the Less, **1065**, and Cyprus, **1066**).

At the close of the twelfth century the reigning prince of Cyprus provoked the wrath of Richard Cœur de Lion by ill-treating the Crusaders. The English monarch thereupon captured the island and sold it to the Knights Templar, who in turn sold it to the French crusader, Guy de Lusignan, titular King of Jerusalem. It was Hugh IV, one of the ablest of the Lusignan dynasty, who was governing Cyprus at the time of the friar's visit. This was the sovereign to whom Boccaccio dedicated one of his works and who brought about an alliance with the Pope, with Venice, and the Hospitallers, which resulted in the capture of Smyrna, in 1344.

After visiting many of the cities of Syria and Palestine, including Jaffa, Acre, Cæsarea, and Ascalon, the friar says of Jerusalem:

"Know that in this Suria (Syria) is the city of Iherusalem, which was sanctified by the holy temple of Salamon (Solomon), built there, and was consecrated by the blood of Ihesu Christo. This land was anciently called Cananea after Canaan, son of Noe (Noah). Afterward it had the name of Judea after Juda, son of Jaco

and reside and they have a flag all white (1081).

Thence I went to Safe (Asafi?) and Azamor. Know that in this province is the very noble city of Marruecos which used to be called Cartagin the Great (Carthage, a mistake in which the traveler confuses Morocco with Tunis). A consul of Rome named Scipio Africanus conquered it in the time of the sovereignty of the Romans. Afterwards the Goths who were the lords of Spain were the sovereigns here. The King of Marruecos has for his device a red flag with a chess-board black and white (1083).

I climbed the mountains of Cueta La-Alta (western Atlas), which is a country well supplied with everything. These mountains are very high and it is a most dangerous land for there are not more than two very perilous passes. The king has for his device a flag—white with a black lion" (1084).

The friar's next objectives were various points along the West African coast as far as the Senegal River traveling always in a panfilo—a galley used in the Mediterranean during the Middle Ages equipped with two masts for sails and one row of oars. He next visited many of the islands in the Canary and Madeira groups. Returning to the mainland he joined a party of Moors who were crossing the Sahara with gold for the King of Guinea. He continues:

"We came to some very great and high mountains in the middle of the Zahara (Sahara) and afterward we traveled a very great distance over the desert until we came to another mountain (oasis?) called Infernent (Zetrain). Here I parted from these Moors and joined some others. I then went to Sulgamenesa (the ancient town of Segelmessa, now Tafilet), a rich city in the Zahara near a river which comes from the clear mountains. The king of it has for his device a white flag with the root of a green palm tree, in this manner (1085).

I went with some Moors over the Zahara until we arrived at Tocoron (Tamegrut on the river Dra) which is a city among some mountains. The inhabitants are negroes and the King of Tocoron has for his device a white flag with a black mountain in the middle like that of the King of Guynoa (Guinea) (1086).

Thence I went to Tibalbert (Tibelbelt south of the Atlas), a city on some very high mountains, thence to another mountain which is under the King of Guynoa (Guinea) and thence to Buda a well-supplied city also on the top of a mountain. Know that the city was peopled by a king of Tremeçen, for he was bad and did evil things and the people wanted to kill him. So he fled with his treasure to this place and founded this city of Buda (on oasis south of Atlas). Its flag is white with a red moon (1087).

Afterwards I departed from Buda and went by the Zahara to another mountain called Genube (Ghana) in which there is a rich well-supplied city of the same name. It is the head of the kingdom where they crown the kings. And the King of Guynoa (Guinea) has a gold flag with a black mountain in the middle (1088).

"Of Guynoa there is much to say. It contains seven mountains well peopled and land yielding abundantly as long as there are mountains, elsewhere it is all Zahara. Two ranges of mountains extend to the Rio Del Oro (Senegal River) and there they collect the ivory teeth and the gold in the ant-hills which the ants make on the river banks. The ants are as big as cats and dig out much earth. This kingdom marches with the Kingdom of Organa (a kingdom on the upper Senegal), in which also there is much desert. Organa is the head of the kingdom where the king is crowned. The King of Organa has for his device a white flag with a green palm tree and two keys (1089).

"I traveled for a very long distance on camels until I arrived at the kingdom they call Tremeçen (Tremizen, or Telensin which extended along the Barbary coast between Melilla and the present seaport of Bougie) which borders on the river Nilus (Nile). They live always at war with the Christians of Nubia and Etiopia (Ethiopia). There are in this kingdom five large places inhabited by negroes. Know that these inhabitants of this kingdom of Tremeçen peopled it from Berberia (Barbary). The king has for his device a purple flag with a white moon (1090).

Thence I went to another kingdom called Dongola (west of Nubia) marching with the deserts of Egipto (Egypt) and the river Nilus. It is a country well peopled with Christians from Nubia but they are negroes. It is a rich land and very well supplied and with many fruit trees. The land has a very hot climate. The King of Dongola has for his device a white flag with a cross like this (1091).

After revisiting Cairo in company with some Genoese merchants whom he met in Dongola the Franciscan journeyed to Damieta (Damietta) where he embarked for Ceuta. He disembarked and journeyed through Morocco, crossed the Atlas Mountains where he met some Moorish traders and embarked with them on a galley for another cruise down the west shore of Africa. "After leaving the mouth of the Senegal River we went on for a very long distance," continues the friar, "always keeping in sight of the coast, leaving behind us the Islas Perdidas (the Atlantic Islands) and came to an island inhabited by many people.

They call this island Gropis (Galpis of the Bissagos group, off the coast of Portuguese Guinea). It is a well-supplied island but the people are idolaters. They took us all before their king and wondered much at us and our language and customs. The merchants who armed the galley made much profit. The king's device is a white flag with the figure of his idol (1092 and 1093).

The Franciscan now left the Moors and journeyed to towns in the Soudan and Senegambia. He marvels at the gold, the ambergris, and the ivory which come from this torrid region and declares that the Mountains of the Moon, also called the Mountains of Gold, are supposed to be the highest in the world and that the five largest rivers in the world have their sources in these lofty regions. He gives

A RED RED SEA

"When the ships come from India they arrive at Aden and pay a tithe of their merchandise, because between the island Aden and the point of Aden there is a rich city. Then there is a very narrow place to pass, and a ship then enters the Red Sea and discharges its cargo at a city they call Sacam (Suakin), belonging to the King of Caldea.

"This Red Sea is so called because the bottom consists of red ochre which makes the water red. By this sea the Jews passed when they went forth from the Egyptian captivity of Faraon the King (Pharaoh). Presently I entered Caldea, which is all surrounded by two very great rivers, rising in the mountains of Toro (Taurus). One is called Cur (a mistake for Tigris) and the other called Eufrates, but not the one of Nubia. Both these rivers reach the Indian Sea in the gulf they call the Black Sea (Persian Gulf). This Caldea is a rich, populous, and well-supplied land.

"Know that in this province is the Tower of Babel, which the giants built in the center of a great plain, the Agra de Senabar (Shinar), and here was the great city of Bauilonia (Babylon), which is now destroyed, of which the lord was Nabucodonusor (Nebuchadnezzar).

"I crossed an arm of the Eufrates and entered the province of Baldaque (Bagdad), in which there is a great city which they call Bandacho (Bagdad), and Nabucodonusor (Nebuchadnezzar) was king of these provinces. I departed from Bandacho and went to Mesopotamia. I left Mesopotamia and went to a city where the river Cur (Tigris) forms a great island called Ansera, in which island there is a great city. Beyond this river is the site of the city of Niniue (Nineveh), which was destroyed for its sins. Know that this region contains very extensive lands, many cities and villages, and is all encircled by the two great rivers called Eufrates and Cur (Tigris). From the borders of the Red Sea to the shores of the Persian Gulf as far as Aquysio (Kishm) we cannot give different devices because Caldea and Baldaque are all in one lordship and it is all one region.

"I crossed the river Cur (Tigris) and made a very long journey until I came to Arabia, traversing a great extent of land and arriving at the city of Al Medina (Medina), where Mahomat was born. Thence I went to Mechan (Mecca), where is the law and testament of Mahomat in an iron chest and in a house of calamita stone. For this reason it is in the air, neither ascending nor descending. Know that this Mechan is the head of the empire of the Arabs. Its device is a red flag and on it Arabic letters in gold (1097).

"I departed from Mecha and traveled over the Kingdom of Arabia onwards until I arrived at a very large city they called Fadal (Fartak), on the shores of the Sea of India. I remained there sometime and then went on board a ship and passed a very large and well-peopled island called Sicocra (Socotra). There is in it a very large city also called Sicocra, under the rule of the King of Arabia. This same island the ships touch coming from India laden with spices. It has a red flag with Arabic letters (1098).

THE WEALTH OF INDIA

"I then traveled with some merchants for a very great distance and arrived at a kingdom of Delini (Delhi), belonging to the kings of India. It contains extensive lands, very rich and populous. The cities I came to were nine. Know that in this Kingdom of Lini (Delhi) the pepper and ginger and aloe ripen, and many other spices, of which there are great harvests, which are taken over all the world. They call this province India the sandy (Sind and Rajputana), and the color of the people is black. They use Turkish bows. They are a wise people, with good memories, and learned in all kinds of knowledge. The device of the king is a white flag with a gold pale (1099).

"I departed from the Kingdom of Dilini and entered that of Viguy (Bijaya-nagar), which is on the other coast of the Indian Sea. Beyond this kingdom there is an island in the Indian Sea called Sagela (Ceylon), in which there is a great and rich city. In this island there are workings whence gold, silver, and other metals and very large rubies come; others smaller. This kingdom marches with the Empire of Armalec (Bengal), with the Kingdom of Linj and with the Indian Sea.

"Know that this Indian Sea is a branch which joins to the great eastern sea. Some say that it covers all the world up to the western sea. Wise men say that as far as the Antarctic Pole there is a great land forming a tenth part of the whole earth. The learned call this land Trapouana (Sumatra), marching with the island of Java and extending to the westward along an arm of the great sea which surrounds the whole earth and of which the Indian Sea is part.

"Know that in the islands of Java and Trapouana there are 45 extensive regions, the greater part desolate, owing to the great heat of the sun. But in the inhabited parts they gather much pepper and many other spices. Here are the great griffins and the great cockatrices. The king has for his device a white flag with a gold wand.

"Afterwards I departed from the Kingdom of Viguy and passed over a gulf of the Indian Sea, which they call the Gulf of Bengala (Bengal), because on its shore is a great city called Bengala, of the Empire of Armelec, and it is the capital of the kingdom. I passed thence to the Kingdom of Oxanap (Burma?), which is on the shore of the Indian Sea. Along the shores of Oxanap the sea is green: it is an arm of the Indian Sea between this Oxanap and the island of Java. The King of Oxanap has for his device a white flag with a pale of gold (similar to Delhi—1099).

"I departed from Oxanap, went on board a ship with some merchants, and sailed over the green sea until we came to the island of Java, a very great island in the Indian Sea about 40 days' journey in length. The island is very populous, but there are no cities, because all the people live in the country and gather spices, pepper, and odoriferous gums. It is a very hot land. The people are black and they adore

(Noah) arrived when it escaped the universal deluge. This mountain is of salt stone as white as crystal. Know that it is one of the highest mountains in the world. No man has been able to ascend it, though attempts have been made many times. These mountains are in the Empire of Persia. All round the country is inhabited by Armenian Christians, who are the guards of the emperor, and he places much trust in them.

"I departed from Armenia and came to the great city of Toris (Tabriz), which is the capital of the Empire of the Persians. It is one of the grandest cities in the world, well supplied, rich, and in a good climate. For this reason the Persians are wise and very well versed in all the sciences. They have learned men with a profound knowledge of the stars. The Emperor of Persia has for his device a yellow flag with a red square in the middle (1105).

"I went over a great part of Persia, going thence to the Kingdom of Saldania and its rich and noble city (Sultanieh?). Its king has for a device a yellow flag with a red square (similar to Persia's—1105).

"I departed from Saldania and went with some merchants a long distance until I came to the city of Ayras (Shiraz), called by the Tartars Sarax, where the Empire of Persia ends. It is a well supplied city, rich and very ancient. They say that in this city was first discovered the astronomy or law of the stars, for this city is in the line of the center of Persia. The cities I have visited in Persia are Casar (Kazan), Serrans, Thesi, Spaor (Ispahan), Jorjaman (Georgia), Spalonero (Razelain), Saldania (Sultanieh), and Toris (Tabriz).

"In this last town is where Besnacayt, the Emperor of Persia, was crowned. His empire extends from the Sea of Sara (Caspian) to the Persian Gulf, where is the city of Hormixio (Ormuz), and from the Mare Mayor (Black Sea) to Aquisio, also on the Persian Gulf. Its length is 125 days' journey and its width from the river Cur to the city of Siras (Sari?) 100 days' journey. Benascayt, Emperor of Persia, assembled a very great host and went to fight with Uxbeco, Emperor of Sara (the Caspian).

"There arrived more than a million and a half of cavalry. Then Benascayt promised some Armenian monks, whom he consulted, that if he won the battle he would become a Christian. The Armenian Christians who came with him marched with a cross before them, and, God helping, he conquered. Uxbeco was defeated and his cavalry pillaged and their women captured. The conqueror advanced far into the enemy's country.

"After this I left Persia with some merchants who came from Catayo (China). Thence we traveled for a great distance without coming to any city, for all the inhabitants lived in the country.

"I came to a city called Tripul of Suria (Syria), which is on the shore of the Mediterranean (not the Tripoli of North Africa, previously mentioned). There I embarked in a ship of Christians and went to Chipre (Cyprus), thence to the Morea, and thence to Creta, Negropont (Eubœa), and a kingdom of Greeks which they call Salonica, bordering on Macedonia, where the great Alexander reigned. The King of Salonica has for his device a red flag with a yellow cross and four chain links (1106).

GALLIPOLI IN AN EARLY CAMPAIGN

"Thence I went to a city called Galipoli, which is on the shore of the gulf between the Mediterranean and the greater sea. By this way the French passed when they conquered Suria. Thence I went along the seacoast to a city they call Recrea (Heraclea), and thence to the city of Constantinople, a rich city, the capital of the empire, where they crown the kings. Here there is a church of God called Santa Sofia, which is very wide, lofty, and beautiful.

"Before it there is a tower of stone which has not been ascended. On the summit of this tower there is placed a knight with his horse of metal. It is very large, and he has on his head an episcopal cap (probably a nimbus or crown). It is in honor of the Emperor Constantine. His right hand is extended toward Turquia, which was formerly called Asia Minor, on the other side of this gulf of the sea. The Emperor of Constantinople has for his device a flag quarterly, first and fourth argent a cross gules, second and third gules a cross, or (gold) between four chain links or (1107 and 1108).

"I left Constantinople and entered the Mare Mayor (Black Sea), proceeding along the coast on the left hand to a great city called Vecina (Vidin). Here nine rivers unite and fall into the Mare Mayor. These nine rivers make a great commotion before this city of Vecina, which is the capital of the kingdom. It has a white flag with four red squares (1109). . . .

"I proceeded along the shores of the eastern side of the Mare Mayor (Black Sea) for a very long distance and arrived in the Kingdom of Sant Estropoli (Sebastopol), which is inhabited by Comanes Christians. Here there are many people who have Jewish descent, but all perform the works of Christians in the sacrifices, more after the Greek than the Latin Church. The king has for his flag—gules a hand argent (1110).

"I left Sant Estropoli and went to Gorgania (Georgia), which is between the Mare Mayor (Black Sea) and the Mar de Sara (Caspian), a very extensive land of the Empire of Uxleto (Uzbeg). I then went along the shore to the city of Trapesonda (Trebizond), where I remained for some time. This empire borders on Turquia, but the people are Greek Christians. The Emperor of Trapesonda has for his device a red flag with a golden two-headed eagle.

"I departed from Trapesonda and arrived at the Kingdom of Semiso (Samsun), a large and populous territory bordering on Turquia and the Mare Mayor. The king has for his device a white flag with a sign like this (1112).

"I came to Feradelfia (Philadelphia) and found a rich and well supplied city. It is in Turquia, anciently called Asia Minor. The king has for his device a flag parted per pale, argent and azure and on a field argent a cross gules (1113).

[illegible]

PENNANTS OF PATRIOTISM 200 YEARS AGO

(Nos. [illegible])

PROBABLY John [illegible]

There are three British ensigns—the white, blue, and red.

To understand the use of the red, the white, and the blue ensign in the British navy, it is necessary to know the organization of the huge fleets of that day. In a fleet there were the center, the van, and the rear.

The admiral of the fleet, with the union flag at the mainmast of his flagship, commanded the vessels of the "center," and they were required to display red ensigns (**1123**), referred to countless times in history as the famous "meteor flag of Old England" on account of its red field and the red cross of St. George. The vice-admiral of the white, with his white flag (**1121**) at the fore of his flagship, commanded the vessels of the van (fore), and they displayed the white ensign (**1124**). The rear-admiral of the blue, with his blue flag (**1122**) at the mizzen of his flagship, commanded the vessels of the rear (mizzen), and they wore the blue ensign (**1125**). So that the ensigns indicated the squadrons, and the colors and the positions (main, fore, and mizzen) of the admirals' flags the ranks of the commanding admirals. This practice was of long standing, and of course came from the English navy, there being practically no Scottish navy. This is all made clear by examination of the admirals' flags, **1121** and **1122**, and the ensigns **1123**, **1124**, and **1125** of the year 1705 (two years before the union of the crosses of St. George and St. Andrew).

At the time of our Revolution the same flags of rank and the same ensigns were in use, but with the union flag of England and Scotland in their cantons. These ensigns continued to have this significance until 1864, when the red ensign disappeared from the place of honor in the British navy, the white ensign (**834**) becoming the exclusive ensign of the navy, the blue ensign (**835**) for public vessels (with a badge in its fly) and naval reserve vessels, and the red ensign (**836**) became the exclusive property of the merchant marine.

The red flag of defiance (**1126**) has for centuries been the symbol of revolution and of mutiny.

Queen Elizabeth chartered the East India Company in 1600. Its flag (**1129**) has peculiar interest for America, as some historians declare that it was the parent banner of our Stars and Stripes. Benjamin Franklin is reputed to have urged its adoption at a dinner which he and Washington attended on December 13, 1775, and at which he is said to have declared: "While the field of your flag must be new in the details of its design, it need not be entirely new in its elements. It is fortunate for us that there is already in use a flag with which the English Government is familiar, and which it has not only recognized but protected. I refer to the flag of the East India Company."

The East India Company's banner at that time was slightly different, however, from the colors shown here (**1129**), for in 1707 the union between England and Scotland took place and the St. George's cross was combined with that of St. Andrew. The East India Company flag vanished from the seas in 1858, when the British Government took over its functions.

The Guinea Company (also a chartered trading organization of England) carried its checkered red and white ensign (**1130**) up and down the West African coast for many years. In 1663 its vessels brought from Guinea the gold from which the first English "guineas" were coined.

The Scottish ensign (**1131**) and Scottish Union flag (**1132**) recall an interesting bit of controversy between the subjects of "South Britain and North Britain," as the English and Scotch were then designated. With the union of the two countries under James I, it became necessary to devise a new flag. A royal ordinance of April 12, 1605, recites the following:

"Whereas some difference hath arisen between our subjects of South and North Britain traveling by seas, about the bearing of their flags,—for the avoiding of all such contentions hereafter, we have, with the advice of our council, ordered that from henceforth all our subjects of this isle and kingdom of Greater Britain, and the members thereof, shall bear in their maintop the Red Cross, commonly called St. George's Cross (**1127**), and the White Cross, commonly called St. Andrew's Cross (**831**), joined together, according to a form made by our heralds, and sent by us to our admiral to be published to our said subjects and in their foretop our subjects of South Britain shall wear the Red Cross only, as they were wont, and our subjects of North Britain in their foretop the White Cross only, as they were accustomed" (see also 829).

The Scottish Union flag (**1132**) carries the quarrel a step farther. The Scottish superimposed the white cross on the English red; the English, on their side, superimposed the red cross on the white.

The Irish ensign at the beginning of the eighteenth century (**1133**) bore the cross of St. George in the canton and a gold harp on a green field, thoroughly appropriate for the "Emerald Isle."

HOLLAND'S FIVE FLAGS

In his "Book of the Universe," Beaumont ascribes five flags to Holland at the dawn of the eighteenth century (**1134**, **1135**, **1136**, **1139**, **1140**). Holland became an independent State in 1579, and in 1599 its flag was officially designated as orange, white, and blue, in three horizontal stripes, these being the colors of the great leader, William, Prince of Orange. In some manner never satisfactorily explained (see 377 and 775), the orange became red early in the seventeenth century, and it was under the tricolor (red, white, and blue) that the naval heroes Tromp and De Ruyter fought their many brilliant sea engagements with the English between 1652 and 1654.

Concerning the city of Amsterdam (**1137**) two centuries ago, Beaumont furnishes the following unique description: "Amsterdam is the most considerable city of all Holland; the houses are generally built of brick, and it's built on piles like Venice. As to what proportion of bigness this city bears to London I have no exact account. Amsterdam for riches, trading, shipping, fair streets, and pleasant habitations scarce yields to any other city of the world. The whole town being in a low

strewn with flower-de-luces or, and Charles VI, who came to the crown in 1380, reduced the lilies in his coat-of-arms to three."

White became the national color of France during the Hundred Years War. Later the Huguenot party adopted the white flag, and when Henry III, himself a Protestant, came to the throne, in 1574, it became the royal ensign. In the following reign (Henry IV) it became the symbol of the French Bourbons. Thus the French ensign (1149), a simple white banner, came to be the basis of many of the French flags (see 1150, 1151, 1157, 1158, 1159, 1160, and 1161). The ensign (1149) was the flag under which Cartier sailed on his voyage of exploration to Canada, and the emblem which floated from the flagship of Admiral De Grasse, whose victory off Yorktown was a most important factor contributing to the success of the American Revolutionary War (see 422). Joan of Arc bore a white flag with gold embellishments at the Battle of Orleans.

The French cornet (1159) is distinctive only in its swallow-tail shape; in modern signaling it is usually called a burgee.

The blue crosses in the banners of Province (Provence) (1150), of Bretagny (Brittany) (1151), and Normandy (1158), and the blue stripes of Picardy (1161) recall the fact that from earliest recorded times until the seat of French Government was removed to Paris (when the red of that city's patron, St. Denis, was adopted) blue was a favorite color of the Franks. It was under the plain blue flag known as "Chape de St. Martin" that Clovis won his great victory over Alaric in 507, and Charlemagne bore it at Narbonne. This was supposed to be the original cloak which St. Martin, while stationed at Amiens, divided with a beggar; the following night he had a vision of Christ making known to his angels this act of charity (see also 743).

Marseilles had a white ensign of its own, with a white cross on a blue square in the first quarter (1160).

The Zealand colors (1152) are, naturally, those of Holland. On the white bar is the distinctive feature, the red lion of the Zealand (Zeeland) coat-of-arms. In the same manner the flag of Middleburgh (1156), the capital of Zeeland, had the colors of Holland, with its own gold tower in the white band.

The Hanseatic League, the famous federation of North German towns which controlled the commerce of northern Europe during the Middle ages, had for its colors red and white, two of the three colors which survive in the flag of modern Germany (996). The chief city of the federation was Lubeck (1153). Hamburg, also an important city of the league, bore a red flag with a white tower (1154), while Bremen's emblem (1166) was a red and white chess-board. Rostock, not content with the league's red and white, added blue (1167), thereby giving her citizens the same occasion as the Russians for complaining that they appeared like "Dutchmen in distress" (see note on the flag of the Tsar of Moscovy—1142).

Dantzick (Dantzic) employed the league's red, but placed upon that field three gold crowns, arranged vertically (1165).

The Munich flag (1164) had an unfortunate color combination, the yellow frequently fading out, leaving the banner a French white (1149).

Lunenburgh (Luneburg) was one of the most important towns of the Hanseatic League. Its flag (1174) included the red field common to Hamburg and Dantzic, but with a winged Pegasus in gold as the distinctive feature.

The flag of Heyligeland (Heligoland) (1155) is of especial interest at this time on account of the tremendously important rôle which the scraps of land (it was one island up to 1720, when a violent eruption of the sea severed a neck of sand and made two islets of it) are playing in the present war as an impregnable naval and submarine base for Germany. Heligoland was a fief of the dukes of Schleswig-Holstein in 1705, but the free city of Hamburg frequently held it in pawn for loans advanced to the dukes. In 1807 England obtained it from Denmark, and 27 years ago made the great mistake of ceding it to Germany.

The Swedish man-of-war ensign (1162) and Swedish merchant flag (1163) 200 years ago were virtually the same as today (826 and 827), with the exception that the blue in the modern standards is of a much lighter shade.

The Genoa ensign (1168) is identical with the St. George's jack (1127).

THE MALTESE CROSS

Few flags of history can rival in romantic interest the red banner with its eight-pointed white cross (1169), emblem of the island of Malta. The eight points of this famous Maltese cross are supposed to represent the eight Beatitudes. In their monasteries the Knights of Malta wore black habits with Maltese crosses over their hearts. In war their coat-of-arms was crimson with the white Maltese cross, like the flag.

The flag of Jerusalem (1170) at the beginning of the eighteenth century contained the same five crosses which the Franciscan monk pictured in 1350 (see 1067), save that the central cross at the later period quartered the flag, and the "Croisettes," as they are called in French, occupied the four quarters.

Tuhen (Thuin, Belgium) was one of several cities of the low countries whose device at the beginning of the eighteenth century was a white swan (1171).

The Danish man-of-war (1172) and merchant flags (1173) are the oldest national emblems now in use, their history dating back to the year 1219, when Waldemar is supposed to have seen a cross in the sky while leading his troops against the Livonian pagans. The flag is known as the Dannebrog (Strength of Denmark). On the time-stained walls of the medieval church on the island of Heligoland there is still to be seen a painted Dannebrog.

The city and district of Surat, the green flag of whose Grand Mogul (1175) was distinguished by two gold scimitars, was the site of the first factory (trading post) established by England in India, a seed which has developed into a great Eastern Empire.

Bengal's Grand Mogul bore a white flag with a red scimitar (1176) two centuries ago. It

THE CORRECT DISPLAY OF THE STARS AND STRIPES

W[illegible]

Photograph by Brown Brothers

INSURING ACCURACY IN A FACTORY WHERE GOVERNMENT FLAGS ARE MADE

The United States Government uses thousands of flags annually, not only the Stars and Stripes and the various flags and pennants of its own army and navy officers and civilian officials, but the flags of other countries as well. Every warship of our navy carries 43 foreign flags, for ceremonial purposes. The flag-maker in a government ensign factory must test all buntings. Sample lots are soaked and washed with soap in fresh water one day and the next in salt water. They are then exposed to weather for ten days, 30 hours of which must be sunlight. The colors must not fade or "run." The material is also tested for its strength. The flag shown above is the Portugal ensign (701).

colors flying, bands playing, and bayonets fixed. It retains possession of the field artillery, horses, arms, and baggage. The French, Russian, and other governments require that in every case the commander of the place must not surrender until he has destroyed all flags; but this must be done before signing the capitulation. General Stoessel destroyed all Russian flags at Port Arthur.

The Hague rules of land warfare forbid the improper use of the flag of truce, of a national flag, or of the military insignia and uniform of the enemy, as well as the distinctive badges of the Geneva Convention. In practice it has been authorized to make use of the enemy's flag and uniform as a ruse, but not during a combat. Before opening fire these must be discarded. Whether the enemy's flag can be displayed and his uniform worn to effect an advance or to withdraw is not settled.

NAVY CEREMONIES OF RAISING AND LOWERING THE COLORS

Shore stations under the jurisdiction of the Navy Department display the national ensign from eight o'clock in the morning to sunset. The same is true of ships at anchor. Ships coming to anchor or getting under way before or after the regular hours hoist their colors if there be sufficient light for them to be seen. Unless there are good reasons to the contrary, ships display their colors when falling in with other men-of-war or when near land, particularly when passing or approaching forts, lighthouses, or towns.

The ceremonies aboard a ship in commission when the ensign is raised and lowered are most impressive. At morn-

Photograph by Paul Thompson

THE LIVING EMBLEM OF OUR NATIONAL UNION

On many occasions and in many places throughout the United States the effective climax of a civic pageant is the formation of a mammoth living flag by school children wearing the red, white, and blue. The great emblem of liberty shown above was formed by the school children of Salt Lake City.

headdress may be slightly raised. The same marks of respect are shown to the national anthems of other countries. At "colors," pulling boats passing near a man-of-war, of any nationality, lie on their oars, and steamers stop their engines, the coxswains saluting and members of the crew outside the canopy standing facing the colors and saluting.

THE USAGES IN FLAG SALUTES

On board ships of the navy it is customary for officers and men whenever reaching the quarter-deck, from aboard boat, from a gangway, or from the shore, to salute the national ensign. They stop at the top of the gangway, or upon arriving at the quarter-deck, face the colors and salute. On leaving the quarter-deck the same salute is given. This is distinct from the salute to the officer of the deck.

When warships enter a port where there is a fort or battery displaying the national flag, or a commissioned ship of war, they display at the main the flag of the country in whose waters they are,

Photograph by Paul Thompson

AMERICAN SCHOOL CHILDREN SALUTING THE AMERICAN FLAG

A sea of hands upraised and a thrilling chorus of treble voices uplifted in salutation as the Stars and Stripes are being unfurled above the newly dedicated Washington Irving High School, New York

© Harris & Ewing

MAMMOTH FLAG BORNE BY MEN WHO FOUGHT TO PRESERVE IT FOR THE UNION

This great banner was carried up Pennsylvania Avenue by veterans of Canton, Ohio, during the reunion of the Grand Army of the Republic, held in Washington, D. C., fifty years after the close of the Civil War. The Dome of Liberty so familiar to all can be seen in the distance.

THE INSIGNIA OF THE UNIFORMED FORCES OF THE UNITED STATES

MEDAL OF HONOR
SERVICE HAT
Worn by Officers in field and all Enlisted Men.
GENERAL OFFICERS . . . . GOLD CORD
ALL OTHER OFFICERS . . . GOLD AND BLACK CORD
RESERVE OFFICERS TRAINING CAMP RED, WHITE AND BLUE CORD
ENLISTED MEN
INFANTRY . . LIGHT BLUE CORD
CAVALRY . . YELLOW CORD
ARTILLERY . . SCARLET CORD
MEDICAL . MAROON AND WHITE CORD
ENGINEERS . . . SCARLET AND WHITE CORD
ORDNANCE BLACK AND SCARLET CORD
SIGNAL CORPS ORANGE AND WHITE CORD
FIELD CLERKS BLACK AND SILVER CORD
QUARTERMASTER CORPS BUFF CORD
SERVICE CAP
All Commissioned Officers
CAP DEVICE
ALL COMMISSIONED OFFICERS
GENERAL (OLD)
GENERAL (NEW)
LIEUT GENERAL
MAJOR GENERAL
BRIG GENERAL
COLONEL
LIEUT. COLONEL (SILVER)
MAJOR (GOLD)
CAPTAIN
FIRST LIEUT
SECOND LIEUT
INSIGNIA OF RANK ON SHOULDER LOOPS COMMISSIONED OFFICERS OF THE U. S. ARMY
(A) REGULARS
(B) RESERVES
(C) NATIONAL ARMY
(D) NATIONAL GUARD
GENERAL STAFF
ADJUTANT GEN'L'S DEPT.
JUDGE ADVOCATE GEN'L'S DEPT
INSPECTOR GEN'L'S DEPT.
QUARTERMASTER'S DEPT.
MEDICAL DEPT
DENTAL CORPS
SANITARY CORPS
VETERINARY CORPS
AMBULANCE CORPS
NURSES CORPS
ORDNANCE CORPS
COLLAR DEVICES COMMISSIONED OFFICERS
A, B, C or D is worn in conjunction with the appropriate corps device
The U. S. is worn on each side of collar and the corps device back of it
OVERCOAT SLEEVES
GENERALS HAVE STARS OF RANK
COLONEL . . . FIVE STRIPS OF BRAID
LT. COLONEL . . FOUR " "
MAJOR . . . THREE " "
CAPTAIN . . . TWO " "
FIRST LIEUT . . ONE STRIP " "
SLEEVE INSIGNIA RESERVE OFFICERS TRAINING CAMPS
SIGNAL CORPS
ENGINEER CORPS
AIDE TO GEN'L
Number of Stars Indicates Rank
CAVALRY
FIELD ARTILLERY
COAST ARTILLERY
INFANTRY
PHILIPPINE SCOUTS
PORTO RICO REG'T
CHAPLAIN
WEST POINT
INTERPRETERS
MACHINE GUN BATTALION
COLLAR DEVICES COMMISSIONED OFFICERS
(See note on opposite side of page)
(A) NATIONAL ARMY
(B) NATIONAL GUARD
(C) REGULAR ARMY
CAVALRY
ARTILLERY
INFANTRY
ENGINEERS
SIGNAL CORPS
QUARTERMASTER CORPS
ORDNANCE
MEDICAL
ELECTRICIAN
WEST POINT MILITARY ACADEMY DETACHMENTS
CAVALRY
ENGINEERS
ARTILLERY
SERVICE SCHOOL
PORT RICO REG'T
PHILIPPINE SCOUTS
DISCIPLINARY BARRACKS (GUARD)
RECRUITING SERVICE
BANDSMAN
MACHINE GUN BATTALION
INTERPRETER
INTELLIGENCE POLICE
Note. A, B or C is worn on right side of collar. On left side is button denoting arm of service.

COLLAR INSIGNIA ENLISTED MEN, U. S. ARMY

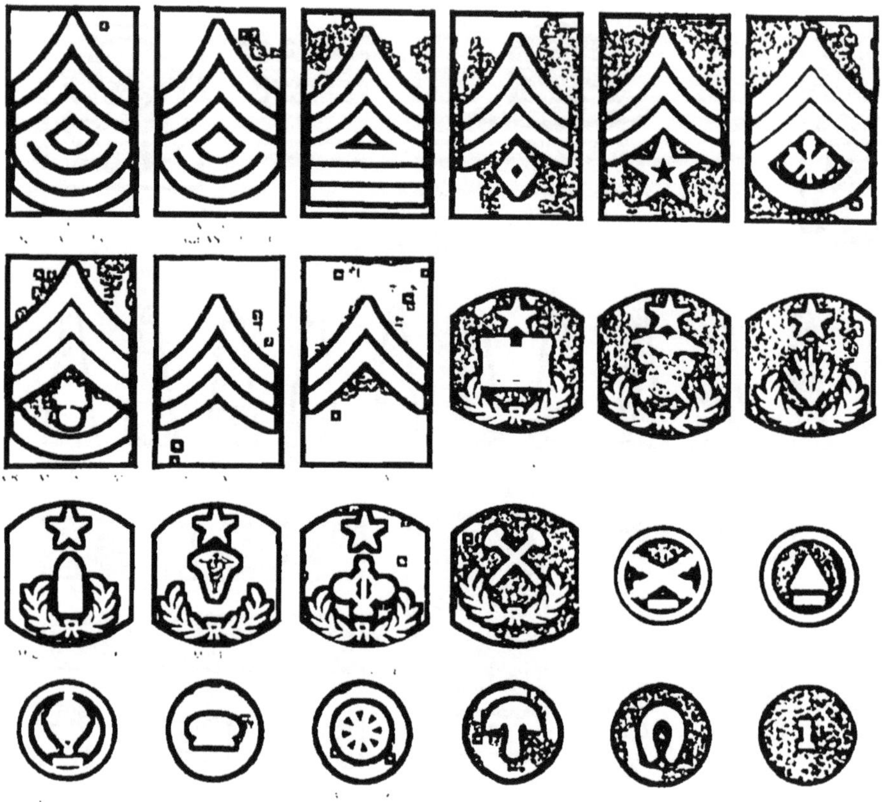

CHEVRONS AND SLEEVE INSIGNIA OF NONCOMMISSIONED OFFICERS AND ENLISTED MEN

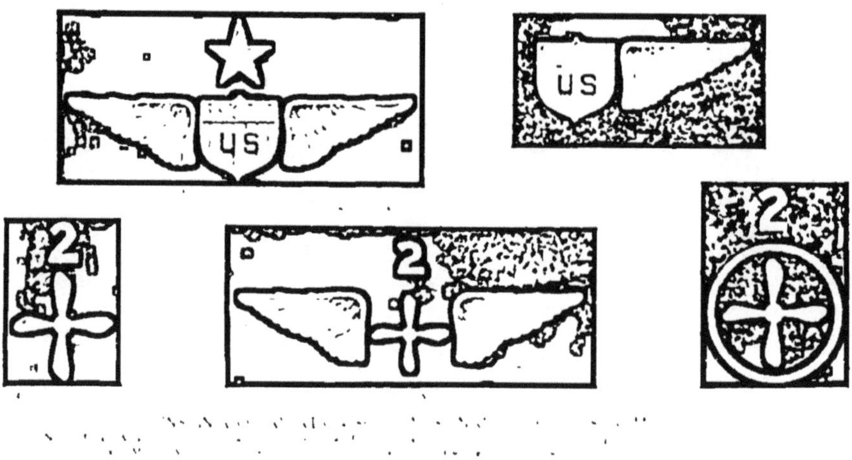

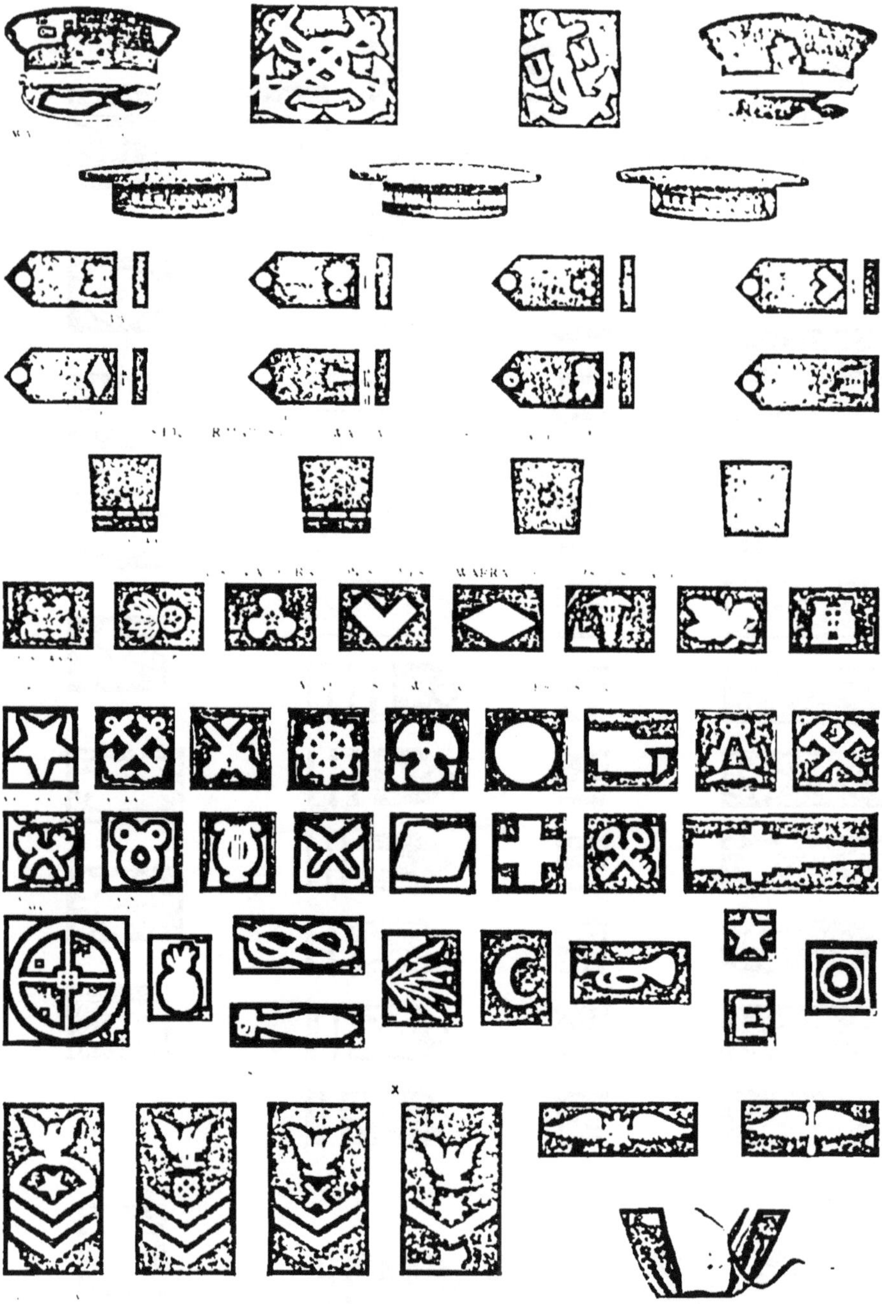

COLLAR ORNAMENTS STAFF AND WARRANT OFFICERS
Staff Officers Wear both Corps and Department Device
Warrant Officers Wear Department Device Only

RANK INSIGNIA COMMISSIONED OFFICERS OF THE U. S. MARINE CORPS ON OVERCOAT SLEEVES

DISTINCTIVE SLEEVE MARKS ENLISTED MEN OF THE U. S. MARINE CORPS

Note. The U. S. Marine Corps follows generally the Insignia of the U. S. Army with the exceptions shown above. Shoulder loop insignia is the same as for similar rank in the army but besides being worn on service coat is also worn on overcoat shoulders

UNITED STATES COAST GUARD

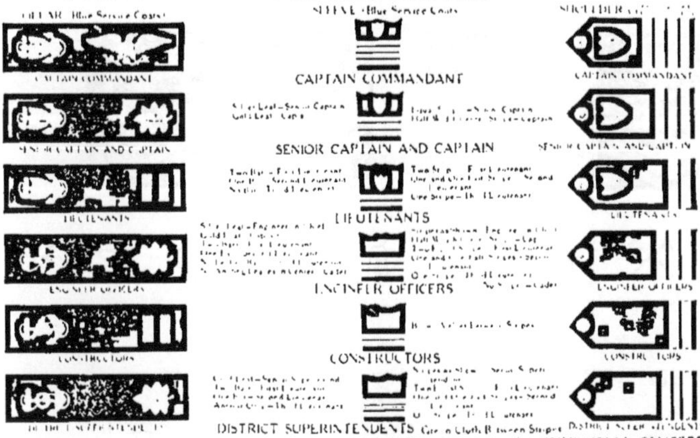

COLLAR SLEEVE AND SHOULDER INSIGNIA OF COMMISSIONED OFFICERS OF THE UNITED STATES COAST GUARD

COLLAR DEVICES OF WARRANT OFFICERS U S COAST GUARD

SPECIALTY MARKS PETTY OFFICERS U S COAST GUARD
(Worn with rating badges similar to those at foot of page 417)

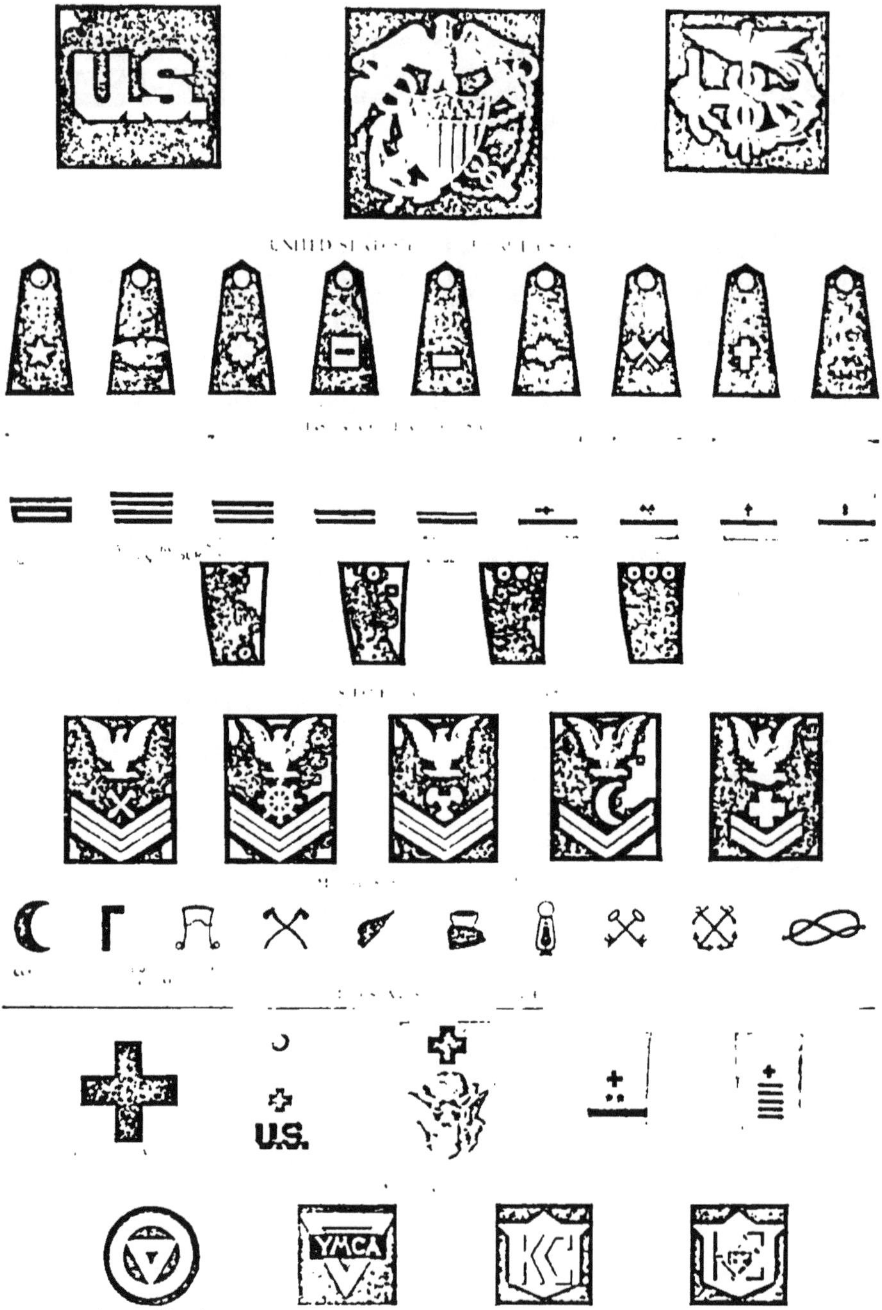
U.S.
U.S.
YMCA

Photograph by May L. Smith

MAKERS OF THE FLAG

Then conquer we must, when our cause it is just,
And this be our motto: *"In God is our trust."*
And the Star Spangled Banner in triumph shall wave
O'er the land of the free and the home of the brave.

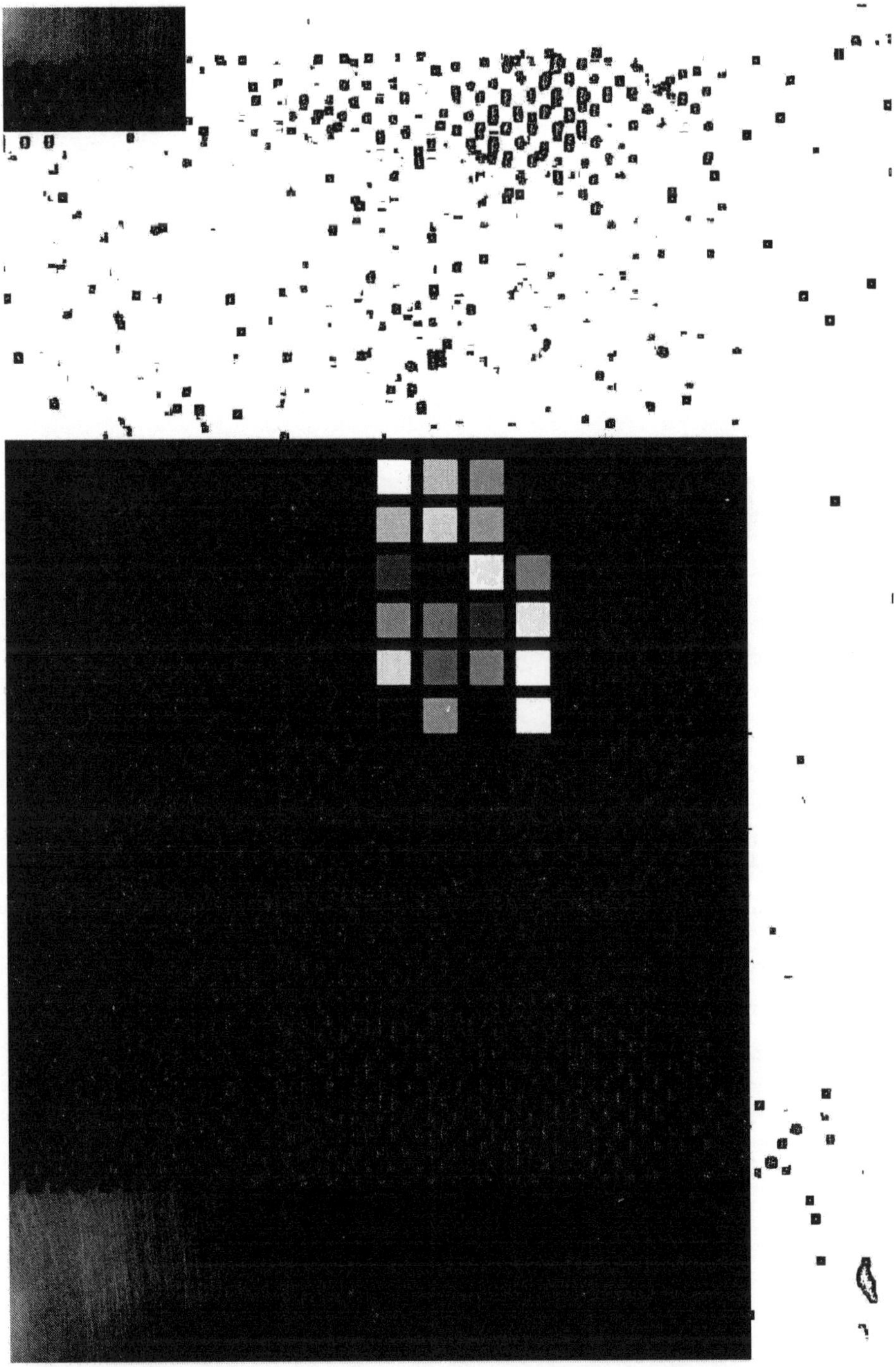

Lightning Source UK Ltd.
Milton Keynes UK
UKHW020634010421
381372UK00005B/500